Aglipayan

The Flourishing of Independent Catholicism in the Philippines

Rev. Dr. Jayme Mathias
Dr. Mercedes Lynn de Uriarte

Extraordinary Catholics Press

Extraordinary Catholics Press
P.O. Box 2386
Austin, Texas 78768

Printed in the United States of America

ISBN 979-8-55-443431-0

Table of Contents

Foreword

Hon. Rev. Dr. Jayme Mathias

For the first seven years of my ministry within the Independent Catholic movement, I knew nothing of the *Iglesia Filipina Independiente*, the Philippine Independent Church, more commonly known by its acronyms in Spanish (IFI) and English (PIC). Then, in 2019, I attended Utrecht University's annual summer school on Old Catholic theology with some 30 classmates from around the world, including Bishop Antonio Nercua Ablon and Father Franz Foerster of the PIC. They spoke of a national church that has served millions and enjoys communion with the Episcopal Church, the Anglican Church, and the Union of Utrecht of Old Catholic Churches. I departed with the impression that our Independent Catholic sisters and brothers in the Philippines are modern-day prophets, courageously witnessing to the gospel amid unfathomable political challenges.

In short, the PIC has accomplished much of what the free-range *clerici vagantes* in the United States have failed to realize: significant growth, the establishment of a national church, and longtime relationships with various ecumenical partners. Imagine for a moment that a series of events led millions of disenchanted Roman Catholics in the United States to seek an alternative expression of Catholicism, that we were able to organize ourselves to collectively meet their needs, and that other churches would want to be in communion with us. That, in essence, is the story of the PIC.

Personally, I'm fascinated by the Aglipayan church, as the PIC is colloquially known, but I also identify with its namesake and first supreme bishop, Gregorio Aglípay (pronounced a-GLEE-pie). Nearly twenty years ago, I wrote a weekly column for a local Spanish newspaper whose editorial team branded me *"el Padre Revolucionario"* ("the Revolutionary Priest") for my emphasis on spirituality over religion—and on our connection with Holy Mystery and with others, over adherence to any institution or tradition. In the truest sense, Aglípay was *el Padre Revolucionario*—or *el Guerilla Padre* (the Guerilla Priest), as he was known as a young cleric. Like me, he served the Roman church as a priest for ten years before the dark underbelly of his church led him to similarly conclude that he could no longer in good conscience serve the papacracy, at which time he served in elected office and helped launch a revolution. Just as the followers of a Nazarean revolutionary eventually assumed his name, as "Christians," our Aglipayan sisters and brothers assumed the name of their founder. We no longer refer to Christianity as a schism in Jesus' Jewish religion, or to Roman Catholicism as a schismatic, heretical offshoot of the Orthodox (or right-believing) church; nor should we attempt to minimize the Aglipayan church by viewing its history only through the lens of those who single out the "sins" of a nationalist "schism" from their ranks, while failing to acknowledge the cruel, racist treatment by their forebears of the Filipino people.

I thank all who helped bring this work together in six weeks, in time for our celebration of World Mission Sunday 2020. Special thanks to my dear friend and mentor, Dr. Mercedes Lynn de Uriarte, for her patience in editing this work. Our second Independent Catholic work together, this book aligns with the themes of our previous works on the history of marginalized school board members in Texas and our most recent book of perspectives on race and racism by school board members throughout the United States.

Special thanks, too, to Carlos Alonso Rodríguez, who incorporated edits into the present work, and to Luis Ordaz Gutiérrez, who shared his graphic design talent to create the cover of this volume. As I'm fond of saying: "Teamwork makes the dream work!"

I also share my gratitude with David and Monica Applewhite, who planted the initial seeds of this work 15 years ago when they gifted me a copy of Ambrose Coleman's *The Friars in the Philippines* and a lovely Filipino stole. Embroidered with a snake and a peasant man, the stole might well symbolize the Roman church's response to the Independent Catholic movement in some places and to the underclass that has largely comprised the Aglipayan church in the Philippines.

This book is a small attempt to bring together several sources on the Philippine Independent Church, so that we in the English-speaking world might benefit from its rich history and fascinating story. May we be inspired by their revolutionary spirit—indeed by the revolutionary spirit of Jesus of Nazareth, who challenged hypocritical religious leaders and overturned the tables of moneychangers in the temple—and join them in creating a more just society and a church that more closely resembles the values that we find in the gospels and in the annals of the Aglipayan church!

Conquest

Five-hundred years ago, on March 17, 1521, Portuguese-born explorer Fernão de Magalhães—more commonly known by his Spanish name, Fernando de Magallanes—arrived on the island of Homonhon, in the present-day Philippines. He claimed the islands he saw for Spain and named them the *Islas de San Lázaro*, the Saint Lazarus Islands. Magallanes and his soldiers sailed on between the larger islands of present-day Leyte and Mindanao. They arrived on the small island of Limasawa, where, according to one account, their Augustinian friars purportedly erected a cross on its highest hill and celebrated their first mass on March 31. Within a month, the residents of the nearby island of Mactan, who resisted Magallanes' novel religion, slaughtered him and his missionaries.

Spain dispatched several other expeditions to the islands, including the 1543 voyage of Ruy López de Villalobos, who named Leyte in honor of Prince Philip of Austria, whose name in Spanish was Felipe Próspero José Francisco Domingo Ignacio Antonio Buenaventura Diego Miguel Luis Alfonso Isidro Ramón Víctor de Austria. Prince Philip would later be crowned king of Spain, Portugal, Naples, Sicily, and the seventeen provinces of the Netherlands. After marrying Queen Mary I, King Philip became sovereign of England and Ireland as well, and his name was extended to the entire archipelago of *las Islas Filipinas*—the Philippine Islands.

In 1565, Miguel López de Legazpi brought some 500 European settlers to the archipelago, to the island of Cebu, and 200 Spanish soldiers arrived two years later. Father Ambrose Coleman, a Dominican friar and Roman Catholic apologist, paints an idyllic picture of his conquering church:

> As Philip was inspired by religious zeal, and his principal and perhaps only object was to spread the light of the Gospel, six Augustinian friars accompanied the expedition. We may say with truth that it was these missionaries, and the others who followed in rapid succession, who conquered the Archipelago for Spain. No conquest occurred in the strict sense of the term. The Spaniards in most places simply showed themselves to the natives; and the religious, who accompanied them, persuaded the

untutored individuals to submit to the King of Spain, through whom they would obtain the two-fold blessing of civilization and Christianity.[1]

Obviously, such reverent submission by "the natives" didn't characterize the 1521 encounter of Magallanes with the people of Mactan. Nor should it be thought to have characterized the conquest of the archipelago through the collusion of the Spanish Crown and the Roman papacracy.

In 1571, the Spanish, with the aid of their Visayan (Filipino) allies and Latin-American recruits—including the Mexico-born *conquistador* Juan de Salcedo—liberated the Maynilan vassals of the Brunei Sultanate, establishing present-day Manila as the capital of the Spanish East Indies. Emboldened by this, 1,500 Visayans joined 400 Spanish and Mexican soldiers and 300 Bruneians to defeat the Muslim Bruneians in the 1578 Castilian War. These allies assisted the defeat of the Japanese Wokou pirates in the legendary Cagayan battles of 1582. In 1588, the Spanish alliance toppled the Tondo Conspiracy, which sought to restore power to an alliance between Japanese pirates and the Brunei sultan. The conspirators were executed or exiled, and Juan de Salcedo continued his conquest of Zambales, La Unión and Ilocos, which included an attack on the Chinese pirate kingdom of Pangasinan. The Christian Spaniards continued their *reconquista* against the Muslim Moors of the islands for 333 years—fathom that—until 1898.

Under a system of *patronato real*, royal patronage of the church, the Spanish Crown assumed responsibility for establishing the Roman Catholic religion in its colonies, with missionaries responsible for the religious conversion and "civilizing" of native populations. In return, the king enjoyed the right to name his friends and allies to ecclesiastical positions at home and abroad. A mutually-beneficial arrangement allowed both the Crown and the Roman church to expand their influence throughout the globe.

Many indigenous people on the archipelago found the new religion very attractive due to the Catholic Church's ritual, pageantry and incorporation of indigenous customs. Similar to its mission systems in Texas and California, the Spanish military built a series of *presidios* or lowland fortresses to protect the archipelago from encroachment by Portuguese, British, Dutch, Muslim and Wokou forces. The Spanish government also sent thousands of Roman

Catholics to the islands: 1,200 Spanish families to Manila, 2,100 soldier-settlers from New Spain (present-day Mexico) to Cebu, Peruvians to Zamboanga City in Mindanao, and *mestizos* (persons of mixed ancestry) to Iloilo, Negros and Vigan.

As was the case in all its distant colonies, Spain struggled to govern the archipelago from afar. The kingdom expended significant resources on its Eighty Years' War with the seventeen provinces of the Netherlands, and nearly bankrupted the colonial treasury of the archipelago through constant warfare with the Japanese Wokou in the north and with Muslims in the south. The Royal Fiscal of Manila recommended that Charles III of Spain abandon the colony, and even the *Real Compañía Filipina* (Royal Philippine Company), which held a monopoly on trade between Spain and the Philippines, closed in 1834 due to financial losses. Intent on winning the entire archipelago for their church, though, Roman Catholic religious orders opposed the withdrawal of Spain from the Philippines. To recoup its losses, the colonial treasury decided to quadruple its revenues through taxation of the Filipino people.

The Cross and the Sword

In his 1493 bull *Inter caetera* (Among Other Works), Pope Alexander VI divided undiscovered lands between Spain and Portugal, assuming spiritual authority over all "discovered" lands himself, but allowing their monarchs to plant the church in those lands in an attempt to maintain colonial governance. Consequently, Spain and Portugal colonized indigenous people through "the cross and the sword," employing military might and the Roman Catholic faith to subdue and "civilize" indigenous people.

In 1899, Dominican Friar Ambrose Coleman penned *The Friars in the Philippines*, a detailed history of evangelization in the archipelago. Though not noting the presence of Augustinian friars with Magallanes' 1521 expedition, Father Coleman shares the following chronology:

- In 1565, two years after the conclusion of the Council of Trent, "the Augustinians were the pioneers in religious enterprise," arriving on the Philippines with Miguel López de Legazpi.[2]
- The Franciscan Friars arrived in 1577, and "the labors of both Orders were so successful that Manila was erected into an episcopal see in 1579."
- In 1579, Domingo de Salazar, a Dominican friar, was appointed bishop of Manila. The Jesuits and Recollects (a.k.a., Discalced Augustinians) entered the archipelago at that time.
- The Dominicans opened two colleges, and the Augustinians opened one, the Poor Clares had a convent with 40 nuns, and religious establishments occupied a third of Manila, largely for the training of clergy and religious for missionary work in the archipelago, China and Japan.

During that time, after the end of the Castilian War of 1578 and the founding of the capital city of Manila in 1579, Pope Gregory XIII placed all Spanish colonies in Asia under the Archdiocese of New Spain (present-day Mexico). Franciscan, Dominican and Jesuit missionaries joined the Augustinian friars in evangelizing the capital city, which was now building a Roman Catholic cathedral and episcopal palace. These religious orders built churches, schools, universities and hospitals in honor of their founders and other Catholic saints. In addition to religion, they instructed native people on the Spanish language, music, and agriculture. As a result of these efforts by church and state, the archipelago became largely Roman Catholic. In Father Coleman's opinion, this evangelization of the archipelago

> was a success to be proud of among a people who, when the missionaries came, had no religious worship, nor temple, nor priest, nor form of worship. They had but a hazy notion of a Deity, their sole religious ideas consisting of some imperfect notions of a hell and a heaven. Persecution only gave zest to the work, [and by the end of the 16th century]…more than six thousand Christians had already been martyred.[3]

Father Coleman shared the following numbers of Filipino converts by various missionaries through 1892[4]:

Clergy/Religious	Claimed Converts
Calced Augustinians	2,082,131
Discalced Augustinians	1,175,156
Franciscans	1,010,753
Secular Clergy	967,294
Dominicans	699,851
Jesuits	213,065
Total	6,148,250

As is evident, due to "the cross and the sword," the archipelago was now becoming deeply Roman Catholic.

The Terror of 1872

By the mid-nineteenth century, calls for rebellion, revolution and independence swept the archipelago, inspired by Latin-American cries for independence. To maintain military control, the Spanish government replaced all non-Spanish military officials with Spanish-born *peninsulares*. This led to the June 2, 1823 uprising of Andrés Novales, which, despite support from Filipino soldiers and from the officers from now-independent Latin American nations, was quickly and brutally suppressed.

Such events spurred the hatred of Filipinos against exploitative *peninsulares* and foreshadowed the "Terror of 1872," a supposed mutiny on January 20, 1872 by 200 colonial troops and laborers at the Spanish arsenal of Fort San Felipe on the island of Cavite. Historians now wonder whether the mutiny actually occurred; regardless, word of the purported event inspired Filipino nationalism. Governor-General Rafael Izquierdo y Gutiérrez blamed the press for unrestrained propaganda inspiring Filipinos to overthrow the Spanish throne. According to his report, Filipino clergy incited a mutiny to establish a new government under Father José Burgos or Father Jacinto Zamora.[5] Spanish historian José Montero y Vidal, sometimes accused of biased storytelling, wrote an account that bolstered Governor-General Izquierdo's telling and stated that the rebels were supported by native clergy.[6] Filipino historian Dr. Trinidad Hermenigildo Pardo de Tavera paints a different picture: that the Spanish friars, whose influence was threatened by the new educational decrees of the Philippine Institute, exaggerated news of a "conspiracy," in order to alarm the Spanish government and pressure Governor-General Izquierdo to delay the reforms that would lessen their influence over the government. Izquierdo happily obliged, blaming a "conspiracy" for his fear-inspiring actions against the Filipino people.

Two days after the purported event, three Filipino priests accused of treason and sedition were executed by garrote — a torturous death by strangulation — for their role in the Cavite Mutiny. Collectively known as GomBurZa, a portmanteau of their surnames, Father Mariano Gómez de los Ángeles, Father José Burgos and Father Jacinto Zamora spoke out for the rights of their fellow Filipino priests and against abuses by Spanish friars. The 73-year-old Gómez de los

Ángeles published the newspaper, *La Verdad* (*The Truth*), 35-year-old Burgos possessed dual doctorates in theology and canon law, and 37-year-old Zamora, a doctor of philosophy, sat beside Carlos María de la Torre, the new governor and captain-general, in the carriage of his inaugural procession — a place traditionally reserved for the Spanish-born archbishop of Manila. Desiring equality with Spanish-born *peninsulares*, the *mestizo* diocesan parish priests warmly welcomed the liberal de la Torre, who was opposed by the conservative, Spanish friars in positions of ecclesiastical power.

Speculation surrounded the shadowy trial and swift demise of GomBurZa. Reports circulated that Spanish prosecutors bribed the artilleryman who testified against the priests. Archbishop Gregorio Melitón Martínez of Manila refused to defrock the priests, because they did not trespass canon law. Instead he ordered the bells of all churches to be rung in honor of the executed priests. Resulting propaganda exposed abuses by Spanish authorities in the archipelago, and Governor-General Izquierdo commuted the death sentences of all other purported mutineers, exiling 20 men — including four priests — to the Mariana Islands (present-day Guam).

Often viewed as the tragic event that sparked Philippine nationalism, the execution of GomBurZa profoundly impacted Filipinos at the time. Dr. José P. Rizal dedicated his second novel, a condemnation of Spanish rule and elite Filipinos, to their memory, writing:

> The church, by refusing to degrade you, has placed in doubt the crime that has been imputed to you; the government, by surrounding your trials with mystery and shadows, causes the belief that there was some error committed in fatal moments; and all the Philippines, by worshiping your memory and calling you martyrs, in no sense recognizes your capability. In so far, therefore, as your complicity in the Cavite Mutiny is not clearly proved, …I have the right to dedicate my work to you as victims of the evil which I undertake in combat.[7]

The Overthrow of Spanish Government
and the Imposition of American Imperialism

In 1892, Filipinos interested in achieving independence from Spain created a secret, alternative Filipino government under the leadership of 29-year-old revolutionary Andrés Bonifacio y de Castro. Later known as "The Father of the Philippine Revolution," Bonifacio fluently spoke Tagalog, Spanish and English. Inspired by the works of Victor Hugo and José Rizal, Bonifacio helped revive Rizal's *La Liga Filipina* (Philippine League), which demanded political reforms in the colonial government of the Philippines. The League disbanded after a single meeting—when Rizal was arrested and deported to Mindanao—but Bonifacio, who organized local chapters of the League in Manila, was soon named chief propogandist.

On the day after the announcement of Rizal's exile, Bonifacio co-founded the *Kataas-taasan, Kagalang-galangang Katipunan ng mga Anak ng Bayan*—or *Katipunan*, for short. A Freemason, Bonifacio infused this secret society with Masonic structures and rituals. Most *Katipuneros* were lower- and middle-class Filipino leaders who despaired of achieving peaceful reform under Spanish rule. In 1895, the Katipunan, which quickly spread through the archipelago, elected Bonifacio its third *Presidente Supremo* (Supreme President). In March 1896, the Katipunan printed a single issue of its newspaper, *Kalayaan (Freedom)*, which contributed to the explosive growth of the organization: from 300 members in March, to over 30,000 members five months later. In early 1896, Spanish intelligence became aware of a seditious, secretive society, but it could not confirm the existence of the Katipunan until August 19, at which time the government began to arrest and imprison suspected traitors.

Three month earlier, on May 3, Bonifacio hosted a general assembly of Katipunan leaders, to debate the start date for the revolution. Officers Santiago Álvarez and Emilio Aguinaldo y Famy warned of a lack of firearms. Undeterred, Bonifacio called an armed revolution against Spain on August 29, the day after publishing a manifesto, which proclaimed:

> It is absolutely necessary for us to stop at the earliest possible time the nameless oppositions being perpetrated on the sons and daughters of the country, who are now suffering brutal punishment and tortures in jails. Because

of this, please let all people know that on Saturday, the 29th of the current month, the revolution shall commence according to our agreement. For this purpose, it is necessary for all towns to rise simultaneously and attack Manila at the same time. All who obstruct this sacred ideal of the people will be considered traitors and enemies, except if they are ill or are not physically fit, in which case they shall be tried according to the regulations we have put in force.[8]

On August 30, 1896, Bonifacio personally led the attack on San Juan del Monte, beaten back by outnumbered but soon-reinforced Spanish troops. While Bonficio's reputation suffered, the revolt spread to surrounding provinces. The greatest success occurred in Cavite, "the Heartland of the Philippine Revolution," which fell within a month to rebel control under the leadership of Mariano Álvarez and 27-year-old Emiliano Aguinaldo. Aguinaldo, whose *nom de guerre* in the *Katipunan* was Magdalo, in honor of Mary Magdalene, became famed for his well-planned victories. Like many others, he quickly tired of Bonifacio's air of superiority—for acting "as if he were a king."[9] Aguinaldo's Magdalo faction of the *Katipunan* scored the first great victories of Filipinos over colonial powers. As a result, the Spanish soon recognized Aguinaldo as head of the rebellion.

In late October 1897, Aguinaldo convened an assembly of generals and established a second, provisional revolutionary government—a constitutional republic. The generals named Aguinaldo president. On December 14-15, 1897, pressured by prominent Filipinos, he signed a pact to end hostilities and dissolve his government in exchange for amnesty and 800,000 Mexican pesos. He and his military leaders departed on December 23 for voluntary exile in Hong Kong.

The February 15, 1898 sinking of the *U.S.S. Maine* in Havana contributed to the U.S. declaration of war on Spain on April 25. By May 1, American Commodore George Dewey defeated the Spanish squadron at Manila Bay. The United States then invited Aguinaldo to return to the Philippines aboard the *U.S.S. McCulloch* to rally Filipinos against the Spanish government. Aguinaldo resumed command of the revolutionary army, and, after a five-hour skirmish on May 28—now Philippine Flag Day—raised the Philippine flag for the first time.

On June 12, 1898, Aguinaldo declared the independence of the archipelago in Cavite, and 12,000 U.S. troops captured the capital city of Manila on August 13. On January 23, 1899, the goal of the revolution against Spain seemed accomplished with the inauguration of Aguinaldo as the first and youngest-ever president of the short-lived First Philippine Republic. The government possessed the first democratic constitution in Asia and a multi-ethnic army renowned for its Filipino officers and racial tolerance.

Six weeks prior, though, on December 10, 1898, the Americans who came to the archipelago as seeming allies brought an end to the Spanish-American War with the Treaty of Paris, which formally handed the Philippines not to Filipinos, but to Americans in exchange for $20 million. This nullified the gains of the Filipino people against Spain, and they now found themselves under the control of another imperial power: the United States of America.

With an air of American superiority, and overlooking the fact that the Philippines had already been Christianized over the course of 377 years, expansionist U.S. President William McKinley—who noted that the Philippines was "a gift from the gods"—declared that since Filipinos "were unfit for self-government...there was nothing left for us to do but to take them all, and to educate the Filipinos, and uplift and civilize and Christianize them."[10] His words rang with the imperialist rhetoric of subduing and controlling other races as "proof that [the human person] had finally passed out of barbarism into true Christianity," and, as was the case in Cuba, the United States would decide the political fate of the Philippines and shape the future course of religion there.

Within two months of the treaty, on February 4, 1899—just two weeks after the formation of the First Philippine Republic—two American soldiers shot three Filipino soldiers, sparking the Philippine-American War, which climaxed in the 1899 Battle of Manila between American and Filipino forces. Aguinaldo was captured by American forces on March 23, 1901, effectively dissolving the First Philippine Republic. On July 1, 1901, U.S. President Theodore Roosevelt named future U.S. President William Howard Taft as Civil Governor of the Philippines. The next year, on July 4, 1902, President Roosevelt unilaterally proclaimed an end to the Philippine-American War on July 4, 1902. Despite these events, the United States did not recognize the independence of the Philippines for 44 more years, until the Treaty of Manila on July 4, 1946.

Setting the Stage for an Overthrow of Church

The Philippine struggle against Spanish colonization set the stage for an overthrow not only of state, but also of the church that exercised dominion over the archipelago for nearly 400 years and was closely identified with Spanish domination. Nature abhors a vacuum: Just as the fifth-century fall of Rome sent the emperor packing to Constantinople, with local bishops and clergy to rule the Eternal City, the distance that separated the Philippines from Spain allowed clergy in the archipelago—the Spanish friars—to assume an outsized role there for centuries. As a result, resentment built among the indigenous and *mestizo* Filipinos toward the Spanish friars, who symbolized the oppression of Spain *and* the Roman Catholic Church. This antipathy often expressed itself in anti-Spanish and anti-friar sentiments. In the same way that Filipinos long desired to overthrow the political power of Spain, they also wanted to now cast off the spiritual power of the Spanish bishops and friars.

The Filipinos possessed a lengthy list of grievances against the Roman Catholic Church, and, as Dr. Daniel Doeppers suggests, "an alien clergy and its temporal role were at the heart of the larger problem."[11] While protesting atrocities committed against the indigenous people, the friars simultaneously purchased great amounts of land from village chiefs, who were happy to sell communal land for private gain. Filipinos now saw the friars as being responsible for seizing their land.[12]

The marginalization and racial discrimination in this polemic were not subtle. The Roman Catholic Church and its religious orders disenfranchised indigenous and *mestizo* people on the archipelago, who were barred from entering religious orders and were not provided the same seminary training as Spanish clergy. After finally allowing their ordination in the 1720s, the Roman Catholic hierarchy blocked the ascent of native and *mestizo* secular clergy, who, despite the fact that they spoke local languages and helped maintain colonial control, were not allowed to serve as pastors of parishes.

The hasty and incomplete training of Filipinos also made them "second-class clergy" in the Roman church, which "magnified the strain between religious and secular priests and tended to debase the indigenous clergy."[13]

14

Due to political turmoil in the 1820s and 1830s, all religious orders in Spain were disbanded — except for those that trained friars for service in the Philippines. As a result, the members of Spanish religious orders fled the anti-friar sentiments of their homeland and came to the archipelago.

Anti-Spanish and anti-friar attitudes soon permeated the archipelago, and Filipino clergy painted the Spanish friars who disempowered them as embodying the darkest tendencies of the Roman church since the Inquisition. Native and *mestizo* clergy pointed, for instance, to the sexual abuse committed by Spanish friars against the Filipino people, making popular a phrase from José Rizal's novel, *Noli Me Tángere* (*Don't Touch Me*) to label the illegitimate child of any Roman Catholic priest as an *anák ni Padre Dámaso* ("child of Father Dámaso"). Ill will abounded. Doeppers writes,

> The Spanish bishops accused their Filipino diocesan clergy not only of ineptitude, avarice, and a "narrowness of soul," but also of inciting anti-friar opinion. They recommended the return of parishes previously assigned to religious curates. While Filipino nationalism and self-esteem produced passion, the intransigence of the friar-prelates exacerbated the situation.[14]

As a result, many native and *mestizo* clergy openly opposed the Spanish government and the Roman church, readily supporting the revolution of 1898.

Ironically, much of the abuse committed against the Filipino people by the Spanish friars is now memorialized in the 1899 work, *The Friars in the Philippines*. Its author, Dominican Friar Ambrose Coleman, countered the "gross calumnies…[and] wicked innuendos" against the "dirty monks"[15] and absolved Spanish friars from all purported sins against Filipinos.

Writing two years after the revolution of 1896, Father Coleman took great effort to explain that "the insurrection [against Spain] was of no ordinary or commonplace nature. It seemed to be directed against the Church, and to be animated by a deadly spirit of hostility to the representatives of Religion."[16] Indignant that the "natives" would show themselves so ungrateful after being evangelized and civilized by the Spanish friars, Father Coleman related an interview of Manila Archbishop Bernardino Nozaleda y Villa, a fellow Dominican friar from Spain:

> When asked what it was that caused the insurgents to be so ferocious against the priests and resolved on their expulsion or destruction, [Archbishop Nozaleda] said the rebels were at once false, unjust, and ungrateful. They had been lifted from savagery by Catholic teachers….The Catholic orders that were singled out for special punishment had planted in the islands the very industries that were the sources of prosperity; and the leaders of the insurgents had been largely educated by the very men whom now they persecuted….It was the antagonism of the Church to murderous anarchy that aroused the insurgents of the Philippines to become the deadly enemies of priests and religious orders. It was true that in Spain, as in the Philippines, the anarchists were particularly inflamed against the Church.[17]

Displaying his characteristic racism and classicism, Father Coleman continued, "The insurrectionary movement was planned, and directed almost exclusively, by the *mestizos*, or half-breeds,—the offspring of the union between native women and the Chinese."[18] He also leveled blame at the *banditti*, "common criminals" who had been released from the archipelago's justice system and who, in his estimation, "burned churches, looted schools and hospitals, treated ordinary ecclesiastical students with brutality, and subjected nuns in convents to shameful treatment."[19]

Father Coleman blamed Protestants, Americans and the press. He, for instance, shared the anecdote of one American Protestant pastor, M.M. Parkhurst, who resided in the Philippines for years and who reported that Roman Catholic missionaries in the archipelago asked for the following stipends: roughly two month wages for a chimney blessing, five months wages for the poll tax, six months wages for a marriage ("so that common law marriages are the frequent result"),[20] and twelve months wages for a "death fee" (i.e., presumably to cover funeral and burial expenses). Father Coleman shared the perspective of a Father McKinnon, who assigned guilt to Aguinaldo and others who revolted against Spain and the Roman church: "Aguinaldo, knowing in his cunning that there were many Parkhursts in America, thought lying about the Church would be an excellent way to gain the sympathy of Americans."[21]

Scapegoated Freemasons

Of all the groups that Father Ambrose Coleman blamed for the war against the Roman church and its Spanish friars on the archipelago—including *mestizo* "half-breeds," *banditti*, Protestants, Americans, and the media—no one, in his estimation, deserved more blame than "secret societies, and, above all, that great guild known as Freemasonry, [which] are certainly foremost, if not controlling, factors in the warfare made upon throne and altar during the last one hundred and fifty years."[22] He wrote:

> The insurrection was a premeditated and deliberate attack made upon the Church by a native secret society which was affiliated to, and adopted the methods of, that type of Freemasonry which gave the Carbonari to Italy and the Jacobins to France; a type whose disastrous work has been so much in evidence in South and Central America. It has unfortunately been busily at work for the last thirty or forty years, indoctrinating the simple natives of the Philippines with the modern watchwords of "Liberty, Equality, Fraternity,"—liberty meaning, in this case, license, anarchy, cruelty, bloodshed; equality, the confiscation of property; and fraternity, an impious combination against all opposed to their designs. And foremost amongst these were undoubtedly from the very first the friars, spiritual guides of nearly six millions of native Christians, who, in consequence of their opposition, drew upon themselves the bitter hatred of the members of the Craft. It thus happened that the friars found themselves denounced and vilified in Spanish newspapers, in circular letters issued at Madrid, in speeches at the lodges and clubs, and in the Cortes [Parliament]. The grossest calumnies, the foulest lies, were industriously circulated, to lower their prestige, and bring about a downfall of that spiritual power they had justly acquired and were exercising for the good of souls.[23]

For Coleman, the toppling of "spiritual power" in the Philippines had antecedents in France, Italy, Spain and Latin America. In his estimation, Freemasons and atheist writers, "aided by the Jansenists, with different motives,"[24] launched the French revolution. They also greatly impinged on the pope's temporal sovereignty in Italy. He continued:

> In Spain, since [Freemasonry's] introduction, it assumed a sanguinary and virulent character; it brought about revolutions and civil wars, embittered classes against one another, wronged and starved the clergy, robbed, turned adrift, and banished the religious Orders.[25]

In Europe, Coleman believed that Freemason indoctrination caused the 1834 Spanish Civil War and the subsequent "onslaught of the religious Orders" on the peninsula.[26] He explained,

> In Madrid, the report was industriously spread by the Masons that the Monks and Friars had poisoned the wells, and were the cause of the sickness among the people. In a mad fit of rage, the populace rose on all sides, rushed to the convents and monasteries, and murdered all the inmates they could lay their hands upon.[27]

Coleman painted a dire picture of precursors in Spain: suppressed monasteries and convents, exiled clergy and religious, the confiscation of church property to finance the Spanish civil war, and the refusal of the Freemason government to pay salaries to all Spanish ecclesiastics. He concluded, "As a result, Spain was filled, in a few years, with a poverty-stricken and starving clergy, and ruined churches and moldering abbeys."[28] Similar actions, in Coleman's estimation, were now being threatened on the archipelago: Manila convents could become barracks and government offices, the schools of the friars could be suppressed, the estates of the friars turned over to the state, and the archbishop exiled.

For Coleman, Freemasons proved themselves the new "missionaries" in the Philippines,

> gathering converts, and strengthening their position, among a class more suitable to their nefarious designs, viz., the *mestizos*, or half-breeds; the Filipinos, or those who, though born in the country, consider themselves the pure-blooded descendants of the early colonists; and the Spanish officials, numbers of whom were already Masons before they went to the Archipelago.[29]

18

In Coleman's estimation, German, English and American Freemasons in the Philippines now conspired against "Spanish interests." He wrote,

> The well-known anti-clericalism of Freemasonry prevailed over every other consideration, blinding them to the fact that the best and most influential representatives of Spain in the Philippines were to be found in the religious Orders, who were the only civilizing force able to deal with the natives. They thus indirectly paved the way for the insurrection; for it is well known that from the ranks of the opposing factions, and principally by reason of their anti-clerical tendencies, arose the sanguinary society of the "Katipunan," which made it its direct aim to expel the friars, and overturn the Spanish government in the islands. The Grand Orient, the organ of this society, declared that one of the first articles of its program was the extermination of the religious.[30]

Noting that 20,000 of the 25,000 Freemasons on the archipelago joined the revolution, often employing Masonic emblems in the branches of the Katipunan, Coleman asked, "Could any clearer proof than this be found that the insurrection in the Philippines is the direct work of Freemasonry?"[31] He also noted the ninth term of the proposal shared by the insurgents with the U.S. government: "There shall be a general religious toleration; but measures shall be adopted for the abolition and expulsion of the religious communities, who, with an iron hand, have hitherto demoralized the actual civil administration."[32]

In April 1898, the superiors of various Spanish religious orders coauthored the "Memorial," a letter to the Spanish government, in which they complained of the insults of former "forsooth" Roman Catholics "who are infected with practical Jansenism of certain latter-day reformers"[33] and of "the crafty insinuation, nay, bold affirmation, already made by the rebel chiefs, that the religious institutes were the sole cause of the insurrection."[34] These religious superiors noted that Pius IX's *Syllabus of Errors* condemned rebellion against civil powers, and they lamented:

> Truly they hate us, and under different names and on diverse pretexts they are making such a cruel war upon us that it would seem as if the Freemasons and Revolutionists

had no other enemies in the Philippines than the religious bodies….They declared they had no dislike of Spanish administration, nor any intention of separation from Spain; what made them rise in rebellion were the abuses of the clergy, and their only demand was the expulsion of the religious Orders.[35]

Blaming Freemasonry as "the principal cause of the social disorganization of the Philippines,"[36] the religious orders shared a passionate plea for the continued alliance between throne and altar. The fearmongering continued: Religious orders were not "a necessary evil, an out-of-date institution which has to be kept up for reasons of state,"[37] but instead required the continued protection of the Spanish government, lest the Philippines should become like Haiti, a "hideous caricature of civilization and Christianity…[where] the history of the black republic is a bloody revolution every two or three years, distinguished by acts of barbarous ferocity…old African serpent-worship, and child sacrifices, followed by cannibalism."[38] These religious superiors unabashedly portrayed their church as a civilizing force, to abet the continued collusion of the Roman church with colonial powers. They also described the leader of the revolution: "Aguinaldo is an ungrateful renegade, who was fed, clothed, and educated by Catholic priests. He is a mere puppet in the hands of the Freemasons."[39]

Antipathy clearly existed between Filipinos and the Spanish friars, and the members of the Katipunan now stood ready to cast off the ecclesial shackles that held their people bound.

From Revolution Against State,
to Revolution Against Church

The Philippine-American War ended on July 4, 1902 with the subjection of the archipelago to the United States of America. Three years prior, the invading power established the Philippine Commission, quickly luring Filipino leaders to collaborate as part of what Filipinos characterized as "the civil counterpart of the invading military."[40] The Philippine Commission, the sole legislative body until the establishment of the Philippine Assembly in 1907, enacted legislation to suppress Filipino aspirations for liberty, including advocacy for independence (1901), armed resistance (1902), support for guerillas (1903), and the display of the Filipino revolutionary flag or the playing of the Filipino national anthem (1907).

Filipino resistance — or, more positively, the Filipino desire for complete independence — continued. To avoid charges of sedition, Filipino journalists, like Aurelio Tolentino, Juan Matapang Cruz, Juan Abad and Vicente Sotto, began to symbolically express Filipino desires for freedom from American imperialism. Revolutionaries like Macario Sakay and the lieutenants of the *Víbora*, Artemio "the Viper" Ricarte, continued their struggle for independence, this time from the forces of American imperialism. Filipinos now channeled their resistance toward the desire for a new, democratic, independent church, free from the grasp of American domination — which valued the separation of church and state.

Leading the movement was Isabelo de los Reyes y Florentino, Sr., the "Father of the Philippine Labor Movement" and the president of the *Unión Obrera Democrática* (Democratic Labor Confederation), which he founded in July 1901. "Don Belong," as he was colloquially known, was a former seminarian critical of the harsh discipline of the Augustinian friars who educated him — and against whom he once led a student strike to protest their mistreatment. He clung to the idea of establishing a national Catholic church independent of Rome, and the American guarantee of religious freedom would now allow for such a dream.

De los Reyes had a long history of advocating for change. In 1889, at age 25, de los Reyes founded *El Ilocano*, the first newspaper written in the Philippine vernacular. After the Philippine Revolution of 1896, de los Reyes, who openly advocated for reform and for the taking up of arms, if necessary, was arrested, charged with being part of Rizal's *La Liga Filipina*, and deported to Spain in 1897. While in prison, he penned his *Memorial sobre la revolución* (*Memorial on the Revolution*), which blamed Spanish friars for sowing the seeds of colonial revolution.

Released from prison in 1898 as part of the Biak-na-Bato pact, but barred from leaving Spain, de los Reyes spent time with the anarchists and extremists he met in prison, studying the writings of European socialists and Marxists. He wrote anti-American articles for Spanish newspapers, and he co-published 86 issues of *Filipinas ante Europa* (*The Philippines before Europe*) against American imperialism. He also penned *La religión del Katipunan* (*The Religion of the Katipunan*), and he translated the Bible to Ilocano as "one way by which [he] could contribute to the liberalization of dogmatic religion."[41]

While in Spain, de los Reyes remained apprised of the plight of Filipino clergy. On January 22, 1899, de los Reyes visited Papal Nuncio Giuseppe Francica-Nava de Bontifè in Madrid, to share the desire of Aguinaldo's government that the Holy See investigate the oppression of Filipino clergy by the Spanish friars. He later wrote in *Filipinas ante Europa*:

> Enough of Rome! Let us now form without vacillation our own congregation, a Filipino Church, conserving all that is good in the Roman Church and eliminating all the deceptions which the diabolical astuteness of the cunning Romanists had introduced to corrupt the moral purity and sacredness of the doctrines of Christ.[42]

During this time, Manila police arrested de los Reyes' brother, Francisco, who was a banker, broker, merchant and Italian consul. According to one news report, the police raided his house and charged him with aiding Filipino insurgents through the distribution of his brother's *Filipinas ante Europa*, published in Madrid.[43]

After a 30-day journey aboard the steamship *Montevideo*, Isabelo de los Reyes stepped foot on the Philippines on October 15, 1901. Ten days later, he appealed to the Philippine Commission for permission to continue publication of *El Defensor de Filipinas* (*The Defender of the Philippines*), which he published during his last ten weeks in Spain. The Commission denied his request. He returned on October 31 to seek permission to form a political party, the *Partido Nacionalista*

(Nationalist Party), to advocate for independence within the framework of U.S. occupation. The Commission again denied his request.

Shifting his attention from politics to the organizing of laborers, de los Reyes formed the *Unión Democrática de Litógrafos, Impresores, Encuadernadores y Otros Obreros* (Democratic Union of Lithographers, Printers, Bookbinders & Other Workers) on February 2, 1902. Neighborhood associations and guilds of cooks, sculptors, seamen, tailors and tobacco harvesters joined this first labor union in the Philippines, causing de los Reyes to rebrand the organization as the *Unión Obrera Democrática* (Democratic Labor Confederation), which possessed 20,000 members by 1903.

Various American newspapers reported on developments surrounding de los Reyes. On March 17, 1902, de los Reyes was arrested on suspicion of planning an anti-government demonstration under the guise of a fundraising event sponsored by Emilio Aguinaldo at Teatro Paz, starring comedian Ernesto Barrenechea. A newspaper article claimed that "nothing was farther from his thoughts than to antagonize the American government."[44] Police officers raided his house and confiscated piles of papers, but de los Reyes was released when no evidence was found to substantiate anti-government activity.

In May, the Associated Press reported that "de los Reyes and the heads of the Filipino workingmen's union are leading an agitation for an increase in the wages of servants, tradesmen, printers, tailors, mechanics, tobacco workers and stevedores [dockworkers]."[45] The next month, the Associated Press reported that strikes in Manila were "growing general…[and] the printers, the butchers, the tobacconists, the hemp workers and the carriage-makers, estimated in all to number over 7,000 men, are out."[46] The article also noted that

> de los Reyes, who organized the strike movement, has become frightened at the conditions which have resulted from his efforts and has resigned the leadership. A dummy leader has been appointed in his stead, but the strikers admit that de los Reyes still issues all the orders. The majority of the strikers tell their employers that they are satisfied with their present wages, which are today three times higher than they were before the Americans came to the islands, but that they must obey orders, as otherwise

they will be killed. When de los Reyes resigned, he said it was a matter of indifference to him whether the Americans shot him on account of his efforts.[47]

All this time, de los Reyes continued his campaign for a national Filipino church. Anti-friar journalist Pascual H. Poblete, a former member of the Katipunan and now President of de los Reyes' *Unión Obrera Democrática*,[48] called a rally of the confederation's general council at the Zorilla Theater on Sunday, August 3, 1902—thirteen days before de los Reyes and four other labor leaders were arrested on the trumped-up charge of ordering the assassination of striking cigar makers if they returned to work at the Commercial Tobacco Factory.[49] Due to bad weather, the afternoon event was canceled.

The same night, de los Reyes, who served as secretary of the organization, called an evening rally at the *Centro de Bellas Artes* (Performing Arts Center), where he announced the formation of a new church, the *Iglesia Filipina Independiente* (Philippine Independent Church). He also shared the names of those involved in the effort.

Dr. William Henry Scott, a historian of Philippine history, shares the following account of that evening:

> In May [1902], nationalist ambitions were at least temporarily quashed by American military might, and in August one of the irate delegates to the Spanish papal nuncio broached the matter of religious independence before a meeting of the first Filipino labor union. "I am fed up with the arrogant attitude of the Vatican towards all demands from our people for justice toward the Filipino clergy," he cried. "I solemnly and without any reservations declare that today we definitely secede from the Church of Rome and renounce allegiance to the Vatican and, relying on God's aid, proclaim ourselves members of a Christian, Catholic, Independent Church, to be ruled and administered by Filipinos!" Those present then proceeded to elect seventeen "bishops" and Gregorio Aglipay as "Supreme Bishop" (*Obispo Máximo*). Thus was the *Iglesia Católica Filipina Independiente* finally and officially born.[50]

Secretary de los Reyes proclaimed honorary presidents for the new church: Governor William Howard Taft, Philippine Commissioner

Dr. Trinidad Pardo de Tavera, and Former President of the Philippine Republic Emilio Aguinaldo. Executive council members included Federalist party leader Felipe Siojo Buencamino, Sr., poet and journalist Fernando María Guerrero, historian and Philippine Public Library creator Manuel Artigas y Cuerva, and *La Vanguardia* publisher Martín Ocampo, who launched *El Renacimiento* (*The Rebirth*) that same day. Secretary de los Reyes also published the names of Roman Catholic priests associated with the movement—Father Adriano Garces, Father J. Barlin, Father Manuel Roxas, Father Toribio Domínguez—some of whom, like Taft and Pardo de Tavera, denied their involvement with the effort. *The Buffalo Times* referred to the nascent church as "a new organization from which everybody is expected to resign…[and which might] create unrest and possibly a clash between the regular Catholics and the dissenters."[51]

De los Reyes named fourteen bishops and proposed a doctrinal council comprised of prominent clergy. He also surprised his friend, Father Gregorio Aglípay y Labayán, with the news that de los Reyes had nominated him to be the church's first supreme bishop.

The Namesake of the Aglipayan Church:
Gregorio Aglípay y Labayán

On May 8, 1860, the province of Ilocos Norte on the island of Luzon witnessed the birth of a boy, christened the next day in honor of Saint Gregory of Nazianzus, who is celebrated by the Roman church on May 9. Gregorio Aglípay Cruz y Labayán, the third child of Pedro Aglípay Cruz and Victoriana Labayán Hilario, was raised in the poor, rural setting of his family. Gregorio's mother died when he was one year old, and he was raised by his maternal grandmother and her children. His brother, Benito, died at age 12, and his older brother, Canuto, later served as chief of police in Victoria, Tarlac, the seat of the revolutionary government. Father Eleuterio José Revollido writes, "Gregorio enjoyed a normal childhood and learned to work hard on the farm with his uncles. As an adventuresome boy he liked to climb the tallest trees and to swim in the dangerous currents of the river."[52]

Various accounts speak of the young Gregorio's first, negative brush with the Spanish colonial government, when he was arrested with an uncle and brought before the tribunal for failing to meet the family's tobacco-planting quota. Such agricultural abuses stirred in Gregorio deep grievances against the colonial Spanish government.

Supported by his uncle, Francisco Amor Romas, who worked for the Dominican Sisters in Santa Catalina, Gregorio moved to Manila in 1879, where he studied under the private tutelage of Julián Carpio for two years. Father Revollido notes one version of the story, which suggests that Gregorio escaped to Manila to avoid a forced engagement, arranged by his father, to a girl he did not love. Though historian William Henry Scott credited the move to Gregorio's desire to pursue education and other opportunities outside of farming,[53] a story of the young Gregorio defying custom could be reconciled with his strong-willed determination to act on anti-Spanish and anti-friar sentiments.

Gregorio enrolled in St. John Lateran College, where he was an average student, before excelling at the University of St. Thomas. Father Revollido writes,

> He could be described as a late bloomer, as seen in his academic records. While he got consistent average grades in his four years at *Letrán*, he blossomed when he

transferred to the University of *Santo Tomás* to become a topnotch student — the historian William Henry Scott puts it, "a topnotch student…[who] took the national prize in psychology, logic and moral philosophy…and served as proctor (*pasante*) in that subject, i.e., a kind of academic master-sergeant who drilled the other students in recitations."[54]

At the University of St. Thomas, Gregorio met several individuals who would later become important Filipino leaders: future revolutionary and Philippine President Emilio Aguinaldo; Isabelo de los Reyes, who later announced the formation of the Philippine Independent Church; "First Filipino Diplomat" Felipe Agoncillo y Encarnación, who represented the Philippines at the negotiations that led to the 1898 Treaty of Paris; Katipunan co-founder Ladislao Diwa y Nocoń; and Marcelo Hilario del Pilar y Gatmaitán, an early leader in the anti-Spanish, anti-friar Filipino propaganda movement. Influenced by his fencing partner, José Rizal, during his last year of studies at St. Thomas, Gregorio decided to enter the seminary, rather than study law.

In 1883, at age 23, Gregorio began his seminary studies for the Archdiocese of Manila. At the seminary in Vigan, 250 miles north of Manila, he studied with Mariano Gaerlan, one of the famous "Nine Clerics" of Nueva Segovia who fought in the revolution, and with Mariano Dacanay, who was tortured by Blessed Gabino Olaso Zabala, a controversy that didn't keep the latter from being beatified by the Roman Catholic Church. It doesn't seem that Gregorio manifested a revolutionary spirit at the seminary, as attested to by his seminary rector, Father Celedonio Mateo de San José, who in 1903 admonished Gregorio:

> "You will not have forgotten those years you spent by my side in the Seminary in Vigan, or of our discussions of theological and moral topics, during which I had the pleasure of hearing your arguments based on the doctrines of St. Thomas….You, Father Gregorio, did not show any inclination to disobedience, much less of rebellion, during the time you were at my side."[55]

On December 21, 1889, at age 29, Gregorio was ordained a priest for the Roman Catholic Archdiocese of Manila. Retired Spanish Dominican bishop Bernabé García Cezón presided over the ceremony at the old Dominican church in Intramuros, 130 miles south of Vigan. Father Gregorio celebrated his first high mass on January 1, 1890 at Santa Cruz Church in Manila.

Like many Filipino priests, Father Gregorio served his entire priesthood as a parochial vicar, or assistant parish priest, to Spanish clergy, in Indang, 35 miles south of Manila (1890); in Nueva Ecija, 80 miles north of Manila (1891); in Bocaue, now a northern suburb of Manila (1892-1896); in San Pablo, 50 miles northeast of Manila (1896); and finally in Victoria, Tarlac, 85 miles north of Manila (1896-1898). In March 1897, Father Gregorio assumed leadership of the local Katipunan chapter in Victoria, where the revolutionary government established itself fifteen months later, in June 1898.[56]

Father Gregorio now found himself in the center of a political and ecclesiastical storm. In the city that served as the seat of the revolutionary government, he employed 30 Katipunan carpenters at his church, and they reportedly saved the forces of Revolutionary General Francisco Macabulos from defeat at the hands of Spanish General José de Lachambre. Because of the young priest's location, Governor-General Basilio Augustín and Archbishop Bernardino Nozaleda commissioned him to plead with revolutionary leaders Mariano Trias, Artemio Ricarte and Emiliano Riego de Dios for the end of the rebellion in exchange for autonomy. On the other side, now back from Hong Kong, General Emilio Aguinaldo sent Colonel Luciano San Miguel to recruit Father Gregorio for the revolutionary army. Archbishop Nozaleda upped the stakes, asking Father Gregorio to travel north to investigate the condition of the bishopric in Nueva Segovia and to secure the release of two Jesuit priests. He obliged. He then decided to join General Aguinaldo's movement in Cavite.

After the establishment of the Revolutionary Government of the Philippines on June 23, 1898, Father Gregorio was elected as a representative to the national assembly of the Revolutionary Congress, which opened in the strategically-located town of Malolos, 25 miles northwest of Manila, on September 15, 1898. Father Gregorio was the sole priest present during the congress' creation of a constitution for the insurgent Philippine Republic, which formed on January 23, 1899.

On October 20, 1898, one month after the convening of the congress, General Emilio Aguinaldo, the president of the revolutionary government, named Father Gregorio his military vicar general — the religious leader of the revolution and the ecclesiastical superior over all Filipino priests. Daniel Doeppers writes, "In this capacity, Aglipay attempted to persuade the Filipino clergy to rally to the support of the Revolution and to seek the Holy See's recognition of a reconstituted church with a Filipino hierarchy."[57]

Father Gregorio stepped into a challenging position. As vicar general, he would harness the moral authority of the church for the cause of the revolution. In the absence of the Spanish friars who chose exile or imprisonment during the revolution, Father Gregorio also oversaw the appointment of Filipino priests to vacant parishes throughout the archipelago. In the absence of hierarchy, he asked each province to elect a lieutenant military vicar to oversee local affairs.

On October 21, 1898, his first full day in his new position, Father Gregorio issued a manifesto, calling Filipinos to organize themselves into a cohesive body prepared for a national emergency. The following day, he issued a second manifesto demanding Filipino clergy to organize themselves, take charge of all vacant parishes, and rally for the revolutionary cause. He wrote,

> The Philippine government, relying on my will and overlooking my lack of merit, has recognized me as *Vicario General Castrense* [Military Vicar General] — that is to say, Chief Ecclesiastical Superior of those under arms during the Revolution. This means, all Filipinos. For this reason, I am likewise Superior to all Filipino priests who, as such, should all be appointed Military Chaplains for the duration of the war.[58]

Riding the crest of popular nationalism, the non-compromising, Masonic revolutionary Apolinario Mabini responded the next day with his own manifesto summoning Filipino clergy to organize their own national church.

On October 23, 1898, Father Gregorio brought together 23 Filipino priests for the Filipino Ecclesiastical Council, more popularly known as the Paniqui Assembly. The priests drafted a provisional constitution for a Filipino church, with no intention of separating from Rome, but rather with the intention of serving a diocese now abandoned by Spanish bishops and friars. Believing the revolutionary cause to be so just that it would be recognized by political and ecclesiastical powers, including the Vatican, the signatories—who didn't count on the support of the parish priest at Paniqui—affirmed that all ecclesiastical authority fell to Filipino clergy.

On November 15, 1898, Roman Catholic Bishop José Hevia Campomanes of Nueva Segovia, who had been taken a political prisoner by revolutionary forces, appointed Father Gregorio— imaginably under some duress—as his diocesan administrator. Historian Tisa Wenger writes:

> Although this appointment conferred only a limited administrative authority, Aglipay leveraged it as far as possible. His installation was a grand affair, complete with parades and a public oath of allegiance before the cathedral in Vigan, that highlighted the continuing importance of the church for the success of the revolution. He held out hope that the Vatican would elevate Filipino priests to the episcopacy and so legitimate the steps they were taking along with the independent status of the Philippines.[59]

As diocesan administrator, Father Gregorio "developed extensive personal ties with the native clergy of the area."[60] On November 26, Bishop Campomanes acceded to Father Gregorio's request that he ordain sixteen former seminarians in Vigan—eight priests and eight deacons—to care for parishes in the diocese that had been abandoned by the Spanish friars. One newly-ordained priest, Father Juan Jamias, later became Father Gregorio's brother-in-law in 1939.

After five months of debate, the Philippine Congress assembled in Malolos in December 1898 to ratify its new constitution. Significantly, President Aguinaldo's chief advisor, Apolinario Mabini y Maranan, made clear in a draft: "The Republic as a collective entity does not profess any determined religion, leaving to individual consciences full liberty of selecting that one which may appear most worthy and reasonable."[61] In the end, religious freedom emerged as a defining principle of the new republic, and not merely as one freedom among a subsequent list of rights. After the constitution's opening declaration on a republican system of government, and before the enumeration of guaranteed rights and freedoms, the founders of the Philippines Republic wrote: "The state recognizes the equality of all religious worships and the separation of Church and State."[62] History Tisa Wenger notes that many devout Roman Catholic congressmen were not entirely convinced of the value of religious freedom.[63] On the one side, Felipe Calderón, who drafted the Malolos Constitution, believed that cutting ties with the Roman church, a possible source of cohesion in the new republic, would cause far too much disruption and would jeopardize their relationship with the Filipino priests who played a central role in the revolution. On the other side, critics pointed out the flaws of the feudal theocracy of the Spanish colonial system, where the decline of Spain was attributed to powerful clergy and the denial of religious liberty. After two tied votes, the article on religious freedom barely passed.

The separation of church and state remained a contentious issue. One representative continued to staunchly oppose religious freedom. He pleaded: "Neither society nor good government can exist without morality, order and authority…and therefore without religion. To permit the liberty of all religions is to concede liberty to both error and impiety."[64] With Mabini, he approached President Aguinaldo and convinced him to suspend the article on freedom of religion and to support the work of loyal Filipino priests. President Aguinaldo knew the influence this man held over priests: The man so staunchly opposed to religious liberty was his military vicar general, Father Gregorio Aglípay.

The Guerilla Priest

Soon proving himself as "an authentic and widely known figure in the struggle for independence,"[65] Father Gregorio was pushed by the Philippine-American War, which broke out on February 4, 1899, to become the *"Guerilla Padre"* [Guerilla Priest]. In this capacity, he led armed resistance as a skilled lieutenant general and tactician, repelling the attacks of American forces in the Ilocos Norte region. Father Revollido notes that Father Gregorio "adopted the classic tactics of hit-and-run raids on enemy garrisons and installations."[66] Despite an absence of love for Father Gregorio in his writings, Jesuit historian John N. Schumacher admitted,

> Aglipay himself was, of course, a guerilla leader of undoubted ability and courage. For almost a year and a half, he carried on guerilla warfare in Ilocos Norte, particularly in the area between Badoc and Batac, but ranging even to Loaog at times. All evidence indicates that he was the soul of the resistance. So serious did the situation become for the Americans that in late August 1900 the American Commander was proposing such drastic measures as declaring the entire male population of the area rebels and treating them accordingly. Earlier, his superior officer, Lieutenant Colonel Howze had reported to headquarters: 'From a very careful investigation in every direction, I find the causes for the outburst to be: first, the fanatical influence Padre Aglipay has over the average man in this province; Aglipay poses and is known as the Filipino government….The greatest number has risen against us because of the fanatical influence Aglipay has over them."[67]

Due to Aglípay's successes, U.S. General Elwell Otis reported that Father Gregorio "by his military operations in the field proved himself to be abler as a soldier than a bishop."[68] The anger felt by American soldiers against the *Guerilla Padre* and his revolutionaries might best be expressed in the words of one U.S. soldier who wrote to his family, "I would rather send a bullet through one of these black-robed, cut-throat robbers than Aguinaldo."[69]

One report by Captain George A. Dodd of the Third Infantry contained the following account of an April 1900 American encounter with Father Gregorio's guerilla fighters:

> Captain Dodd's force, consisting of 87 men and 93 horses, left Vigan, the capital of Ilocos Sur province, on April 8, and headed northward. Early on the morning of the 15th, his command encountered a large party of insurgents under Gregorio Aglipay in the mountains near Badoc. In a fierce fight, lasting an hour, 49 insurrectos were killed, four were mortally wounded, and 44 were made prisoners. The affray took place in a thick jungle, which made the movements of the soldiers very difficult.[70]

According to the report, another 120 insurgents were killed the next day, with only a spear wound inflicted on one of Captain Dodd's sergeants. With 169 deaths to zero, one might wonder whether American newspapers were reporting more than facts, or whether Father Gregorio's guerilla fighters were so unprepared for war against U.S. forces.

Father Gregorio was portrayed as a leader in the Filipino struggle for religious independence, following in the footsteps of the martyred GomBurZa of 1872 and advocating for recognition of the Filipino clergy who received the same formation, education and ordination as Spanish clergy. He perceived himself to be thoroughly Catholic, as is expressed in his first manifesto of 1899:

> Because of our sacred ministry, we are called to defend in these islands the immaculate purity of the Catholic religion. It is very necessary that we take advantage against the avalanche of impiety which always takes politico-social disturbances to infect the purest tradition.[71]

He echoed this sentiment of Catholic purity, free from foreign domination, in his second manifesto:

> The Revolution, having triumphed and the independence of our Motherland having been solemnly proclaimed by a regularly-constituted government, patriotism imposes on us, in the first place, the duty to acknowledge it as *fait accompli* inasmuch as we clearly see that its purposes, as regards the Catholic religion that the Filipino people profess, tend to preserve it in all its purity; and we must

not only recognize it but we must incorporate it by means of our forces and in consonance with the character of our mission to the effective realization of its noble ends without doubting even for a moment that those ends were and are to liberate our people from foreign domination.[72]

On April 29, 1899, within three months of the outbreak of the Philippine-American War, Archbishop Bernardino Nozaleda—a Spanish Dominican friar who believed Filipinos incapable of self-governance and who forbade his priests from supporting the revolution—excommunicated Father Gregorio for usurpation of ecclesiastical jurisdiction (i.e., for assuming the title Military Vicar General). Father Gregorio, in turn, declared Archbishop Bernardino Nozaleda excommunicated for collaborating with Spaniards and Americans to starve and abuse the Filipino people, for supporting an unjust colonial regime, and for betraying Christianity itself by imposing racial distinctions on people.

After the capture of President Emilio Aguinaldo by U.S. forces on March 23, 1901, Father Gregorio surrendered to American troops in April 1901. Dr. Scott notes that "the greatest compliment to his reputation as a patriot was unwittingly paid him by General J. Franklin Bell after the Ilocano surrender [who] requested permission to keep one cavalry unit in the field in case the *Guerilla Padre* changed his mind."[73]

Having suffered military defeat, Father Gregorio continued his campaign for the right of Filipinos to govern the Philippine church. Relations with the Roman church continued to quickly sour, particularly now that Apostolic Delegate Placide Louis Chapelle, arrived in the Philippines on January 2, 1900. A Frenchman, the former archbishop of Santa Fe and of New Orleans quickly turned Filipinos against him and his church with his pro-friar, anti-Filipino rhetoric, which suggested that Filipinos were only capable of menial positions of responsibility in the Roman church. Historian Tisa Wenger writes:

> [Archbishop Chapelle] had begun his ministry in the racially-segregated worlds of Baltimore and Washington, D.C., and brought with him the racial sensibilities of the American South. Much like Nozaleda, he believed Filipinos incapable of managing their own parishes, let

alone a diocese or a nation. Chapelle convinced U.S. governor-general E.S. Otis that the Spanish friars should be permitted to return to their former parishes, at least until American priests could be appointed to replace them. Filipino Catholics thus found themselves under the ecclesial authority of an archbishop who came to them from yet another imperial power and considered them racially incapable of governing themselves.[74]

Some suggest that Chapelle's less-than-diplomatic manner of speaking facilitated future schism with the Roman church. Two disappointed Filipino priests, Father Salustiano Araullo and Father José Chanco, attempted to travel to Rome, to plead with the pope for change, but the war impeded this.

Whereas the priests gathered at the Paniqui Assembly desired to remain part of the Roman Catholic Church, Father Gregorio now dialogued with American Protestants about a possible alliance to establish a Filipino-run church.[75] Homer Stuntz, a Methodist bishop, wrote an extended account of his first encounter with Father Gregorio:

> In October, 1901, Aglipay called all the Protestant ministers in Manila to a secret conference in the rooms of the American Bible Society….He disclosed to us at that time his plans with some fullness of detail, and wound up with the modest (?) proposal that we should all merge our work into his, gain the immense numerical strength which he was confident he could command, and then leaven it with the truth….We pointed out to him the essentially negative character of his program and urged him to seize the great advantage afforded by his unique position to give those who should follow his lead something better than a mere rallying cry "against Rome." We urged particularly that he give great prominence to the Bible and the reformation of the lives of all who followed him—priests and people. He pleaded the necessity of not going too fast for his [Roman Catholic] constituency, [and] the danger that they would think it a Protestant movement….We were all pledged to secrecy, and I think the pledge was kept inviolate by all who listened with such absorbing interest that day to this anti-Romish plot.[76]

The idea of separating from Rome was gaining momentum, and Father Gregorio spoke of this possibility with other priests and wartime comrades on the occasion of his 42nd birthday, on May 8, 1902, at a gathering now known as the Kullabeng Assembly.[77] He also dialogued about it with his old classmate from St. Thomas University: Isabelo de los Reyes, Sr., of the *Unión Obrera Democrática.* With the imposition of U.S. imperialism, Father Gregorio found himself out of work, without a position in the now-defunct Philippine Republic, and excommunicated by the Roman Catholic Church. Little did he know he would soon be put to work by his friend, "Don Belong."

On August 3, 1902, de los Reyes surprised Father Gregorio—not only with the announcement of the formation of a new nationalist church, the *Iglesia Filipina Independiente* [Philippine Independent Church], but also with the news that he had nominated Father Gregorio as the nascent church's first *Obispo Máximo* (Supreme Bishop).

Like all Filipino priests, who were now forced to decide whether they would support or rebuff de los Reyes' dream, Father Gregorio had to discern which path he would choose. Nearly two weeks later, on August 16, 1902, he wrote a circular which went public four days later, in which he advocated for exhausting all means of reconciliation with Rome before declaring schism. The following day, the *Manila American* derided de los Reyes' Philippine Independent Church as "the church that died before it was born."[78]

Undeterred, de los Reyes formed the church's executive committee, comprised of friends from the *Unión Obrera Democrática.* He printed circulars and the church's first "fundamental epistle." In response to Roman Catholic Bishop Martín García y Alcocer's denunciation of the separation, de los Reyes published his second "fundamental epistle," encouraging members not to render evil for evil, but making clear that revolutions can be in accord with the will of God:

> Neither the leaf of a tree nor a single bird falls to the earth without the will of our Heavenly Father (Mt. 10:29). Revolutions, therefore, are perfectly providential, and despite their causing us momentary disasters, they ultimately bring us far-reaching redemption and result in benefits that will bless many generations to come. They are

like typhoons which, in the twinkling of an eye, destroy and erase secular vices and abuses, and their social upheavals, moreover, have this time been used by Divine Providence to castigate the errors of an enthroned frailocracy, errors over which we now wish to draw the veil of merciful oblivion.[79]

Brave women and men began to join the revolution, aligning themselves with de los Reyes and against the Roman Catholic Church and its Spanish frailocracy. José Rizal submitted the membership applications for Saturnina Bunda and 62 fellow residents of Navasota. Then a watershed moment then occurred when Father Pedro Brillantes, the ecclesiastical governor of Ilocos Norte, "accepted and solemnly joined our holy church, and this gave great impetus to the religious movement."[80] As a result, several priests and seminarians began joining the new church, as well as a number of lay persons from several municipalities, guilds and labor unions, "and even expatriates."[81] Twenty-four of twenty-five former Roman Catholic priests in Ilocos Norte participated in Father Pedro's consecration as a bishop on October 1, 1902.

In contrast, Father Gregorio showed an interest in preventing schism. Though he had committed grave acts of insubordination — like declaring his own archbishop excommunicated! — he showed no intention of separating from the Roman Catholic Church. Instead, he continued to dream of an indigenous clergy under the authority of the pope.

Father Gregorio accepted the invitation of Jesuit Fathers Francisco Foradada and Joaquín Villalonga to speak about the matter at the Jesuit house in Santa Ana, Manila. Professor María Christine Halili relates the episode:

> For four days, Fr. Francisco Foradada, a Spaniard, exerted all efforts to win back Aglipay to the Catholic fold, although the latter had not yet given up his Catholic faith. On the fifth day, Foradada handed Aglipay a document for his signature, affirming his return to Catholicism. Aglipay wanted an assurance that, by signing the document, the problem of the Filipino Catholic priests will be solved, that is, their appointment to the posts formerly held by the Spanish regulars. Foradada in return replied why did he mind so much Filipino priests, considering they are vicious

an inefficient. Aglipay felt very offended and he demanded Foradada to withdraw his odious remark. He left the Jesuit house and severed relations with Roman Catholicism.[82]

After more than a month of discernment, Father Gregorio left the Roman Catholic Church and joined the Philippine Independent Church.

The First Supreme Bishop

1902-1940

Father Gregorio Aglípay decided to live the American promise of religious freedom, which was now dawning in the Philippines. The Federal Party heralded his decision, offering a glowing review of his actions in the pages of its newspaper, *La Democracia* (*Democracy*):

> The die is cast! Padre Aglipay has crossed the Rubicon of intransigency and absolutism, with the decision and energy of a Roman captain….It is the assertion of the dignity of the people, the last consequence of the revolution, which, in order to be complete, requires religious liberty.[83]

Historian Tisa Wenger writes:

> "Freedom of worship, freedom of conscience, and liberty of action" had finally come to the Philippines. At long last, the Catholic Church was seeing "the political and religious effects" of its former abuses. For the Federalists, the new church signaled the end of the Catholic monopoly under Spain and the dawn of true democracy and religious freedom in the Philippines.[84]

On September 6, 1902, nearly five weeks after de los Reyes' announcement of the formation of the Philippine Independent Church, Father Gregorio was consecrated a bishop by fellow priests. Nearly 50 years later, a PIC Supreme Bishop explained:

> The secession from Rome was on such a vast scale that the necessity for immediate organization moved Mons. Gregorio Aglipay to accept consecration as *Obispo Máximo* on January 18, 1903, at the hands of those who lacked regular episcopal consecration….He accepted such consecration on the grounds of expediency and because the urgency of the times prevented his going to Europe for investiture at the hands of bishops of the Old Catholic Church.[85]

On October 1, 1902, the day on which Bishop Brillantes took possession of the newly-created Diocese of St. James the Greater by occupying a Roman Catholic church in Ilocos Norte and declaring it his cathedral, Father Gregorio signed the short-lived 1902 Constitution of the Philippine Independent Church. Other signatories included PIC Secretary General Isidoro C. Pérez and others who accepted de los Reyes' nomination as bishops. Homer Stuntz, a Methodist bishop, provided a "free translation" of the preamble to the PIC Constitution:

> With the purpose of having a Filipino national Church, independent of Rome, similar to those organized in the past, which today are acknowledged as (belonging to) the greatest and most civilized nations of the world—England, Germany, Russia, Italy, France, Greece, Belgium, and America; and moved by faith in the biblical principal that God, with His Son, our Savior, Jesus Christ, is the Founder of all Christian societies in all places which have dignified humanity, lifting it above the wretchedness of sin, of slavery, and of barbarism; we, the faithful Christians of this Filipino people, of our free and spontaneous will, have resolved, by common consent, to found, and hereby do found, our Church, for which we establish and approve this constitution.[86]

Bishop Stuntz also chronicled the events that transpired after the signing of that constitution:

> An inner coterie got together, adopted a constitution, elected Aglipay "Obispo Maximo," or archbishop, elected more than a score of the Filipino clergy throughout the islands bishops, and set the date for the first public mass. That was held in Tondo, one of the subdivisions of Manila, where hostility to the friars is so great that no friar has set foot there since the American occupation. Mass was finally said in the street, and was participated in by a very large number. Then the people in another part of the city call Pandacan…invited him to occupy their old and well-appointed (Catholic) church. Their priest denounced the effort from the pulpit, only to receive such a pummeling as must have opened his inner vision, if it did close his outward organs of sight. And it was administered by women! They declared that he insulted them by his allusion to certain reasons why the people preferred

Aglipay to himself. These irate women took their beds and cooking utensils and literally lived in the yard surrounding the church…and anti-Aglipaites had scant welcome there for several days of furious excitement. Aglipay and his followers calmly claim practically all the churches in the Philippines![87]

Historian Tisa Wenger shares the same story, but with more detail:

In one case where a loyal [Roman] Catholic priest had criticized Archbishop Aglipay, a mob of women threw the priest to the ground, tore off his cassock, and invited Aglipay himself to say Mass in their church. During the few weeks, the women actually slept in the churchyard to prevent the offending priest's return.[88]

Wenger suggests a "doctrine of peaceable possession" prevailed, with the person holding the church keys determining whether that church would be used by Roman Catholics or Aglipayans.

On October 20, 1902, in accord with de los Reyes' first fundamental epistle, which justified the consecration of Filipino bishops, Father Gregorio was consecrated Supreme Bishop by his brother priests. In Supreme Bishop Aglípay's catechetical exposition of the sacraments, he later provided the theological justification for the consecration of bishops by presbyters or priests:

There is absolutely no biblical text that prohibits or invalidates the consecration of a Bishop by a Presbyter. On the contrary, the Presbyters consecrated the first Bishops for the simple reason that there was no Bishop, as that word is yet to be found in any gospel.[89]

On October 26, Aglípay celebrated his first solemn pontifical mass as Supreme Bishop, where de los Reyes' third fundamental epistle, the "Declaration of Principles"—the first epistle signed by the Supreme Bishop—was shared. According to the IFI History Committee, several thousands of people attended the Mass in an open field.[90]

Three days later, de los Reyes published the PIC's fourth fundamental epistle, which outlined the organizational structure of the church, a prescribed curriculum for theological education, and immediate steps to remedy the archipelago's need for priests.

Supreme Bishop Aglípay declared November 2, 1902 as a day to commemorate heroes of the Philippine Revolution, including José Rizal and GomBurZa. That day, clergy and laity of the PIC took over Roman Catholic churches in Paco, Pandacan and Sampaloc. On November 9, the municipal council of Lagonoy passed a resolution renouncing its allegiance to the Roman Catholic Church and declaring its councilmen and parish priest as members of the PIC.

On November 10, 1902, Philippines Governor William Howard Taft reported that the PIC could "have an important bearing upon future conditions and which may perhaps add much to the labor of maintaining of peace and order in the archipelago."[91]

On November 16, 1902, in light of the rapid growth of the PIC, Supreme Bishop Aglípay issued a statement explaining the rationale for a new church:

> The time has come for a Filipino National Church for the Filipino people, ministered by the Filipino clergy. Years of friar oppression made this imperative. The liberty of worship and conscience and the separation of Church and State could make it contemptible for us to give spiritual allegiance to the Italians in Rome claiming temporal power whose recognition from government by all means known to masters of deception.[92]

On December 8, 1902, de los Reyes published his fifth fundamental epistle to protest Leo XIII's September 17 apostolic constitution, *Quae mari sinico*, which was later promulgated at the Roman Catholic cathedral of Manila on December 8. The apostolic constitution articulated a vision for reorganizing the Philippine church after the flight of Spaniards, who left 80% of the parishes in the archipelago vacant. Supreme Bishop Aglípay fumed that, through the apostolic constitution, the pope awarded "all ecclesiastical titles" to Spanish friars and addressed Filipino clergy "as if dealing with savages." He wrote, "Instead of pacifying us, this Constitution will make the Filipino clergy shake off the Roman yoke."[93]

By the beginning of 1903, civil authorities in the Philippines agreed that four Spanish religious orders should withdraw from the archipelago during the next two years, leaving more parishes to Filipino priests and religious.

On January 18, 1903, the PIC bishops of Isabela, Cagayan, Pangasinan, Abra, Nueva Ecija, Cavite and Manila re-consecrated Supreme Bishop Aglípay, thus manifesting their obedience to him. Three days later, the PIC launched publication of a new newspaper, *La Verdad* (*The Truth*). By February, Filipino poet and playwright Aurelio Tolentino was speaking in PIC parishes, making the first references of the PIC rising from the ashes of the Philippine revolution.

On May 14, 1903, Supreme Bishop Aglípay asked Governor William Howard Taft to hand over the Roman Catholic cathedral in Manila, noting that ownership of ecclesiastical properties was granted by royal and papal decrees to the Spanish government (now replaced by the U.S. government), that all churches on the archipelago were constructed through Filipino labor, and that the archipelago no longer recognized the spiritual authority of the Roman church. The Roman Catholic hierarchy, of course, countered that its churches did not belong to the people, but instead to the organization for which they were built. At the time, Methodist Bishop Homer Stuntz shared:

> [Aglipay's] plea is that [the churches] were built by public funds "for the religious use of the Filipino people," …and that their use is to be settled by an appeal to the people. These claims were urged and answered by Aglipay and the representatives of the friars before Governor Taft, and he decided that, as one of the regular [Spanish] clergy had been "in peaceable possession" when the fray began, he must be reinstated, and if Aglipay and his people wished to push the matter of their claim, they must institute regular proceedings in the courts.[94]

Though rebuffed by the governor, Aglípay began a five-year campaign to acquire nearly half of all Roman Catholic properties in the Philippines — some through considerable bloodshed.[95] By 1904, Aglípay claimed that half the population of the archipelago belonged to his church.

On August 17, 1903, de los Reyes published his sixth and last fundamental epistle, which addressed human freedom and included scathing attacks on American occupation of the archipelago:

On September 17, 1903, in accord with the nationalistic spirit of the nascent church, Supreme Bishop Aglípay canonized four Filipino heroes — José Rizal and the GomBurZa — stating that they were not to be venerated with idolatrous honor, but seen as examples of courage and heroism to imitate.

On October 11, de los Reyes, who just returned from Japan, published the first issue of a new publication, *La Iglesia Filipina Independiente Revista Católica* (*The Philippine Independent Church Catholic Magazine*).

On October 28, 1903, the PIC adopted its *Doctrina y Reglas Constitucionales* (Constitutional Doctrine and Rules), which, slightly revised in 1918 and 1940, served as the PIC's doctrinal foundation and rules of governance through 1947.

On December 1, 1903, Bishop Eduard Herzog of the Swiss Independent Church recognized the new church, writing of its common denominator with Old Catholicism: "We conserve the Catholic Faith, Catholic Sacraments, the Catholic Liturgy and the Catholic Constitution" — but independent of the Vatican.

On June 26, 1904, Bishop Aglípay penned a letter accepting the invitation of Roman Catholic Apostolic Delegate John Baptiste Guidi to attend the Roman Catholic Provincial Synod of Manila on August 7, 1904. One source writes:

> Bishop Aglipay's letter also expressed gratitude to this conciliatory gesture, especially since it did not contain the usual fulmination and menacing phrases [from the Roman church]. However, he wanted to know if the synod would be willing to discuss the motives which had driven the Filipinos to that painful separation.[96]

In many ways, Aglípay's church resembled the Roman church. Sixty years before the liturgical reforms and inculturation of liturgy recommended by the Second Vatican Council, Aglípay's priests celebrated Roman Catholic rituals, though in Spanish or Tagalog, rather than in Latin. They also employed forms of worship that expressed the culture of the Filipino people. The Aglipayan church taught Roman Catholic doctrine — except with respect to the "universal supremacy" or purported "infallibility" of the pope. This was expressed in the PIC's 1902 Constitution, which stated that "the dogma and the creed [of the new church] shall be the same as those professed by all apostolic Catholic Christians, with the exception of obedience to the Pope."[97] Aglipayans celebrated Mass and engaged in Catholic traditions, including the veneration of saints canonized by the Roman church prior to 1902. The architecture of their churches also mimicked Roman Catholic temples.

Early Aglipayan Periodicals

As a journalist and publisher, Isabelo de los Reyes shared his gifts with his Aglipayan sisters and brothers, providing their church a voice — both within the Philippines and abroad — and assisting them with the development of their identity as Aglipayans.

The first Aglipayan newspaper appeared on January 21, 1903, with the same name as the famed newspaper of GomBurZa member Father Mariano Gómez de los Ángeles: *La Verdad* (*The Truth*). The church published 29 issues, through August 5, 1903. Methodist preacher Arthur W. Prautch edited the work, with the assistance of Manuel Xerez-Burgos. Prautch stepped down after 12 issues, and Xerez-Burgos assumed editorship, with the assistance of Lázaro Makapagal.

The second Aglipayan periodical, edited by Isabelo de los Reyes, appeared on October 11, 1903. *La Iglesia Filipina Independiente Revista Católica* (*Catholic Magazine of the Philippine Independent Church*) saw 55 issues and concluded on December 15, 1904. One of Isabelo's sons became editor of the work beginning with the fortieth issue, as Isabelo traveled outside the Philippines. This periodical was distributed "in the whole Philippines," as its header proclaimed, alongside *La Redención del Obrero* (*Redemption of the Working Person*), a 20-issue publication by de los Reyes from October 8, 1903 to February 18, 1904.

The first issue of the *Revista Católica* stated its aspiration (*Nuestra Aspiración*):

> We sincerely aspire to make a periodical that deserves the designation of Christian because of its love for God, because of its profound respect for the sacred things, because of the charitableness that can be felt in all of its lines….It would be a vile deed if we were hoping that our success would lie in systematically fighting against the Romanists, exploiting the passions of our coreligionists and dividing our compatriots that profess different religions more and more….We therefore make a formal promise that if those of other religions do not throw the first stone, we will live in sacred peace with them; and that even if they do fight with us, that we will know to contest them with measure and always with the charity that our Divine Master teaches us.[98]

These early Aglipayan periodicals were indeed a method of throwing "stones" back at those who hurled them. Former First Philippine Republic Prime Minister Pedro A. Paterno, for instance, wrote in his newspaper that, presuming Manila Archbishop Jeremiah Harty carried through with his promise to elevate Filipinos to the highest ecclesiastical positions, "the Aglipayan schism obviously loses all of the foundation that supports it."[99] The following week, de los Reyes published an article entitled, "Anemic Spirit and Head":

> The one who is really VAIN and RIDICULOUS is the author of that sorry paragraph, to try to ridicule our respectable compatriot priests; perhaps only to flatter the friars....Before you judge our Church, you should first have studied its Doctrines and constitutional Rules, which have been published already. Effectively, we follow all the evangelical dogmas of the Roman Church; but not Rome's invented dogmas, especially those that are opposed to the believers educating themselves about the sciences, even if this means that they have to read the theories of authors who are serious but [also] pantheists, Darwinists, rationalists, Protestants, atheists, etc. We also don't follow the dogmas invented by Rome that precisely contradict the clear words of the New Testament....I want to say, instead of intransigent, obscurantist, tyrannical, hypocritical, or excessively fussy priests, we would like to have educated priests who do not fear the light of the modern sciences....In summary, we follow Roman Catholicism in all which is serious in it and where it conforms to the modern sciences; but not in placing obstacles in the way of their free development; that is, a Catholicism that reasons freely.[100]

In his response, de los Reyes also noted that the Roman Catholic Church alone refused to acknowledge the legitimacy of the Philippine Independent Church and its Supreme Bishop. In a tit-for-tat war of words, the Dominican friars of *Libertas* (*Liberty*) fired off a response two days later in the Roman church's defense:

> Nervous and irascible, [Isabelo] reeled off a "letter"....So excited is Isabelo about his schism, that he believes that the whole universe is stunned with admiration for this new "Independent Church"; and he is outraged because Mr.

> Pedro has called it a "vain and ridiculous sect"....That all the Churches, minus the Roman, have recognized and praised the Aglipayan church! How the foreigners are pulling your leg, poor Isabelo![101]

These early publications were important tools for disseminating doctrine, sharing Aglipayan history, and offering an Aglipayan apologetic. After a year of publication, Supreme Bishop Aglípay reflected in the *Revista Católica:*

> In this collection are found the Catechism and the rest of the doctrines, the rules, the history, and the most solid defense of our church in all questions, and this organ has certainly arrived to fill a gap, not only to defend us immediately against all the intrigues of our implacable enemies, but also to contradict in an irrefutable way those who would spread something of the sort that we do not have proper doctrines or rules, but only a ridiculous parody of Romanism or the sects.[102]

As a publication by revolutionaries — within church and state — early Aglipayan periodicals walked a fine line, desiring to liberate oppressed Filipino clergy and laity, but not wanting to be perceived as being political or, worse, as a revolutionary force within the American colony. Roman Catholic propagandists attempted to discredit the Aglipayan church as purely political. Father Edward Vattman, the senior Roman Catholic chaplain of the U.S. Army, for instance, fueled fears of Aglipayans in seditious, anti-American cloaks of religion who "instilled a spirit entirely foreign to submission to American rule."[103] The *New Zealand Tablet* similarly wrote that "the wretched Aglipay has tacked religion to the draggled skirts of his political scheme,"[104] adding a week later that Aglipayans comprised "a rowdy and turbulent political movement."[105] Moving their coverage up in the paper, to ensure reader attention, they pressed:

> We described [Aglípay's] "movement" as "almost wholly a political one , both in its methods and its aims...."Bishop" Aglipay's schismatic movement is degenerating into a triangular political combination with the Workingmen's Union and the Nationalist Party, and...is absorbing a majority of the irreconcilables in the Nationalist

> Party....Aglipay has practically made no change in the doctrine of Catholics beyond refusing to recognize the Pope. The future of the movement will probably be largely political.[106]

In 1904, even the Philippine Commission judged the Aglipayan church to be "political rather than religious," and with a "motive [that was] another insurrection."[107] Dominican Friar Ambrose Coleman, who previously bolstered the racial hierarchy of the Roman Catholic Church's colonial efforts, now wrote of Aglipayanism as a "form of Oriental fanaticism" and "simply a phase of the revolt of the Yellow against the White man."[108]

Within this context, the Aglipayan *La Verdad* deflected attacks, pointedly stated that "the Filipino national Catholic church is a fact," and rooted the church's actions in the U.S. values of religious liberty and freedom of conscience. *La Verdad* went even further, likening the Aglipayan church's struggle to the American Revolution and noting that, in the same way that the Anglican Church became the Episcopal Church of America, the Roman Catholic Church of the Philippines had now become the Philippine Independent Church.[109]

Knowing that the word "independent" marked the church's very name, and clarifying that the PIC did not seek political independence from the United States, *La Verdad* pointed out:

> The label "Independent," which our Holy Church carries, has absolutely no political meaning....Our Holy Church started to adopt the label of "Independent," that is independent of Rome, just so that it cannot be said that we are deceiving the people. When this period of propaganda is over, it will be possible to eliminate it. But this label never had any — and never will have any — political meaning.[110]

Nine months earlier, on the cover of the first edition of *La Verdad*, de los Reyes sought to assuage concerns that Aglipayans constituted a revolutionary movement: "Never will a line appear in *La Verdad* that questions the sovereignty of the United States in these islands. That point being definitely settled, the political future must be worked out with this as a basis."[111] Later in the issue, de los Reyes clarified,

> It is essential that all Filipinos convince themselves of the necessity of being independent in religious matters and of not being slaves or tributaries to a power that, taking the

name of God, only does this to unite in its sphere the money of all nations.[112]

Adrian Hermann writes of this tension experienced by de los Reyes, who knew that others would attempt to discredit Aglipayans as "political," as an extension of the revolutionary spirit that characterized the Philippine Revolution of 1898, or as being a danger to the social order of the young American colony. Any of these could threaten the survival of the young church. Even Independent Catholics in Gao, in western India, could see the potential danger that occasioned their January 1905 letter to Independent Catholics in the Philippines:

> We know that the government of the United States will qualify your church as a "Center of Anti-American Subversion"…and that all the sacrifices that Monsignor [Aglípay] took on himself in the foundation of his great Independent Church will be reduced to NOTHING, and we foresee its fast disappearance; and as Monsignor will understand, with this disappearance, the Roman Church will return to triumph.[113]

Importantly, early Aglipayan publications also connected the church with the world, and vice versa. Established in the 1880s, the Independent Catholic Church of Ceylon, Goa and India remained in communication with Supreme Bishop Aglípay for over eight years. Swiss Old Catholic Bishop Eduard Herzog wrote to Supreme Bishop Aglípay, encouraging him with the news of national Independent Catholic churches in Switzerland, Germany, Austria and the Netherlands. They exchanged communications and periodicals for nine years, until Bishop Herzog rejected the PIC catechism and severed communications with Supreme Bishop Aglípay. Archbishop Joseph René Vilatte of the American Catholic Church also shared with the PIC his spiritual support. Such communications were published in Aglipayan periodicals as "another evident proof of the affections" (*otra prueba evidente de las simpatías*) of other Independent Catholics throughout the world for Aglipayan clergy and laity.

As is evident, Supreme Bishop Aglípay encouraged his followers to read far more than the periodicals of his church. He encouraged the study of modern science, and, according to Bishop Stuntz, he purchased and distributed 25,000 copies of the Bible to Filipinos.

Realizing how Aglipayans were receiving the word of God in a way that would soon allow Protestantism to outpace Aglipayanism in the Philippines, Bishop Stuntz, who saw many advantages in the "indigenous Filipino Reformation" that was the Aglipayan church, wrote, "Aglipay loosens this fruit from the tree, and we gather it."[114]

Early Growth & Contraction of the Aglipayan Church

The early Philippine Independent Church quickly grew, and, at its zenith in 1904 to 1905, one-quarter to one-third of the Christian population in the archipelago self-identified as Aglipayan.[115] Historian Tisa Wenger suggests that one tenth of Filipino priests left the Roman Catholic Church and brought their congregations into the Aglipayan church.[116]

Dr. Daniel Doeppers traces the geography of Aglipayan adherence, showing that the largest percentages of Aglipayans lived in the northern Ilocano region of the island of Luzon — the birthplace of de los Reyes, Aglípay and Brillantes — or were Ilocano migrants living in Manila.[117] Doeppers notes that higher numbers of elite and average citizens alike joined the Aglipayan church in that region He also suggests that clergy in the region chose the Aglipayan church more readily than other clergy for other reasons: Native priests in their diocese of Nueva Segovia were less likely to serve as pastors in parishes, and, because they graduated from the only seminarian on the archipelago not run by the Vincentians, they were less grounded in Roman Catholic theology and ecclesiology. The Aglipayan church quickly diffused from there, "aided by popular indignation about the Holy See's failure to provide a Filipino hierarchy and to withdraw the friars."[118] Parishes were established in neighboring Pangasinan, then farther south in Zambales and Tarlac — two regions where more than 75% of Catholics self-identified as Aglipayan. Doeppers also notes a "'boondocks factors," "a tendency for the PIC to be more successful in out-of-the-way places."[119]

In 1903, Methodist Bishop Homer Stuntz wrote on the growth of the nascent Aglipayan church:

> The movement went forward with astonishing rapidity. Aglipay now claims three million adherents, though he admits that this estimate has no accurate statistical basis, but is founded upon reports. There is no denying that it has become formidable. City after city and province after province have declared with much emphasis that they are for Aglipay and for freedom from *"El Papa"* (the Pope) and from all those whom he appoints.[120]

In January 1905, Supreme Bishop Aglípay inaugurated a new, prominent, national cathedral, which stood on a half-acre lot at present-day 227 Claro M. Recto Avenue in the Tondo district of Manila. After the death of the church's first pastor, Father Félix de la Cruz, in 1907, the Tondo Cathedral was served by several clergy who later figured prominently in the PIC, including Supreme Bishop Santiago Fonacier, inaugural PIC Secretary General Isidoro C. Pérez (the bishop of Cagayan and an early leader of Filipino clergy along Aglípay), and Bishop Manuel N. Aguilar, a later Secretary General who received apostolic succession alongside Supreme Bishop Isabelo de los Reyes, Jr.

The very name of the Aglipayan cathedral—for the Holy Child of Tondo—was an act of resistance against colonial and imperial powers: Stories circulated of an indigenous, pre-Hispanic Holy Child (*el Santo Niño,* or *Salbadur Sunu* in Eskayan), who brought Christianity to the archipelago long before the arrival of Spanish explorers and revealed the superiority of indigenous language and belief, over Spanish dogma and the Latin language.[121] The indigenous narrative accommodated Aglipayan rejection of Rome and appropriation of church property—symbolized in Eskayan folklore as the stealing of a white bell [likely symbolizing the color of the Spaniards' light skin] from the tower of a mission church by the *Santo Niño* reincarnated as a bird.[122] The nationalist Aglipayans were the present-day Eskayans, invulnerable to Spanish muskets and seizing Roman Catholic missions! The Spanish would later disparagingly mark Aglipayans with the Visayan term *dyusdyus* ("false god," a reduplication of the Spanish *Dios*), which they had previously used of the *Santo Niño*. In the Eskayan legend, the imperial forces are not vanquished, and the unbaptized rebels flee into the forest where they continue their acts of resistance. As an apt metaphor for Aglipayans, Piers Kelly might be paraphrased: "Today, many [Aglipayans] see themselves as direct successors of [the *Santo Niño's*] rebels, the unbaptized Boholanos who, having fled into the forest, never submitted to foreign rule."[123]

The flight of the Spanish friars from the archipelago during the 1898 Philippine revolution against Spain created an immense opportunity for Aglípay and his clergy. As native and *mestizo* clergy, they were now able to pastor congregations, taking advantage of abandoned Roman Catholic churches to better serve the spiritual needs of their faithful. The Roman Catholic Church, on the other hand, found itself "reduced to the status of a foreign mission, dependent in every way—for funds, for [people], for leadership—on foreign aid."[124] All five Spanish Roman Catholic bishops departed the archipelago by 1903, and Pope Leo XIII, "displaying an imperial disdain for the capacities of colonial subjects,"[125] transferred episcopal responsibility to the American church, which chose four American bishops and a Filipino apostolic administrator for the archipelago.[126] Historian Tisa Wenger notes, "In the eyes of many Filipinos, these appointments mocked their aspirations and dismissed the capability of the native priests."[127]

Under U.S. imperialism, the Aglipayan claim to Roman Catholic properties proved premature. The Vatican sued the nascent church and cajoled the U.S. government—which already viewed the Aglipayan church through a lens of rebellion and revolution—to pressure the Philippine Supreme Court to rule in its favor. On July 24, 1905, the Philippine Commission enacted Act 1376 to address the ownership controversy that resulted—not only for churches, but also for convents, schools and cemeteries. On November 30, 1906, the Supreme Court handed down a momentous decision ordering the PIC to return all properties that formerly belonged to the Roman Catholic Church. The case was appealed all the way to the Philippine Supreme Court, where it was upheld in 1909. A rapid decline in membership followed, leading to the Aglipayan church's first significant contraction.

Ten years after the creation of the Aglipayan church, Roman Catholic apologists continued to defame the PIC and its leaders. One example in the United States was published by *The Catholic Advance* of the Roman Catholic Diocese of Wichita. Though far removed from the archipelago, its editorial staff went to great lengths to dissuade its readers from considering any action resembling those of the PIC. The paper painted the picture of the "agitator," de los Reyes, returning to the Philippines in 1909 "with the object of rehabilitating the Aglipay sect for political purposes."[128] The "power behind the bamboo throne," de los Reyes continued to be a threat to the Roman church, now that he had

> returned partly to save the sect from a death by inanition, and partly upon the recommendation of Ramon Diokno and Felipe Buencamino of the *Unión de Trabajo*. By reviving the PIC, de los Reyes hopes to advance the cause of

independence. He has shrewdly concluded that the best way to sway the Filipino people is through religion. He thinks that if he can make the sect powerful throughout the islands, that it will not be difficult to convince the people that it is but a step from religious independence to political and national independence. In this work, de los Reyes will have the sanction of Aglipay and assistance of several ambitious spirits. The basis of the campaign will be the fact that Assemblyman Dimas Guzmán of Isabela was buried according to the sect and directed, when he died last March, that his funeral services be of the Aglipayan order. The Philippine Assembly gave him an official burial in the marble hall of the *Ayuntamiento* and, over the protest of Roman Catholics, Aglipay conducted the services clothed in his purple robes. This occurrence will be used by de los Reyes and his friends to show the Filipino people that Aglipay and the PIC has been officially recognized by the Philippine government. [129]

Methodist Bishop Homer Stuntz also chronicled early responses to the early Aglipayan church. "The spread of this movement has maddened the friar element beyond all expression," he wrote. "The vials of their wrath have been poured out upon all and singular who joined the movement or gave it aid or comfort."[130] In the same work, Bishop Stuntz shared an example of the scathing attacks by Roman Catholics against early Aglipayans, this from Roman Catholic Bishop Martín García y Alcocer of Cebu, the apostolic administrator of the vacant see of Manila, who ordered that the following words be read from all Roman Catholic pulpits:

Have you not heard, and perchance comment upon, the latest project of the new heresiarchs? Christian instinct and even the simplest common sense has impugned as a farce and a crazy imposture the project of a national Church independent of the Holy Roman Church. The Filipino people know very well that outside the true Church of Jesus Christ, which is, without a reasonable doubt, the Roman Catholic Apostolic Church, there is no possibility of salvation. It knows that all schism and sectarianism is a rude separation from the true Church—dry branches cut from the tree of the cross, a rebellious and disobedient faction, a banner of treason, a misled society without order, without hierarchy, and without possible union. To enter the fold of sectarianism is to leave the sweet and holy law of God and of the Church to follow the caprices and tyrannies of any rebellious chief. Schism means for the people a real slavery which will bind with chains, apparently of gold, the destinies of the country to the whims of sects. This is an error so monstruous that we can scarcely comprehend it. It is wishing to do two things in themselves contradictory. One cannot be a Catholic without obeying the Roman pontiff, who is the vicar of Christ, the successor of St. Peter, and the legitimate superior of the Catholic Church. A Catholicism without the lawful Pope, who is the Pope of Rome, would be a phenomenon as monstruous as it is ridiculous and perverse. Outside the roman Church, there is no possible Catholicism.[131]

Bishop Stuntz rightly concluded: "The mind of one who could seriously issue such a paper would make an interesting study in religious psychology."[132] Even today, some Roman Catholics overlook the beam of their own schismatic, heretical history — excommunicated in 1054 A.D. for tampering with the Church's ancient creed and for their innovations of leavened bread and clerical celibacy — to draw attention to the speck in the eyes of Independent Catholics, who seek to reclaim a more genuine history of the Church. The persecution endured by our Aglipayan sisters and brothers more than a century ago was nothing new; nor has it yet been sentenced to the annals of history.

A Nationalist Church

The Aglipayan church, often romantically idealized as "the most tangible product of the 1898 Revolution against Spain,"[133] embodied the intense nationalism that accompanied the war for independence and the strong anti-Spanish and anti-friar sentiments of the Filipino people. As a result, the Aglipayan church soon espoused the nationalist and democratic values that its founders held dear. Following the democratic, lay-led model of the Executive Committee proposed by de los Reyes, Supreme Bishop Aglípay empowered lay leadership of the church, in line with "the most pure democracy and universal confraternity" that inspired the first apostles to magnanimously love, forgive and share their possessions with all, thus allowing them to live in "the most beautiful and radiate freedom."[134]

For the Aglipayan church, the Filipino struggle for independence in matters of church and state accords with the will of God, who desires liberty and freedom for all. Suffering the effects of Spanish domination for centuries and American imperial during the four years leading up to the founding of the PIC, the writers of the church's Fundamental Epistles and *Doctrinas y Reglas Constitucionales* (Doctrines & Constitutional Rules) wrote:

> Our Church is Catholic or Universal, for it considers all [people] equally children of God, and it bears the designation "Philippine independent" to identify this association of free [persons] who, within the said universality, admit servility to no one.[135]

On May 21, 1909, the Philippine Assembly approved a resolution ratifying its desire for eventual independence from such colonial powers as the United States. In honor of this event, the PIC created an annual nationalist celebration, its Mass in Honor of Heroes of the Revolution, first celebrated on June 4, 1910. The preface of the Mass included a supplication to God for "freedom, independence and solace," a phrase popularized by the Katipunan. Beginning in 1911, the liturgy incorporated the patriotic "Hymn of Glory," a product of the archipelago's Hiligaynon people, which was translated to Tagalog.

After the creation of this national day, Supreme Bishop Aglípay issued statements exhorting all clergy and laity to advocate for their independence. He defended his clergy against those who suggested that the Aglipayan church should stay out of Philippine politics, noting that, "beneath their robes, they are Filipinos."

The intense nationalism of Aglipayanism rings in the church's motto: *Pro Deo et Patria* (for God and Country). Father Dionito Cabillas suggests that the "unity, mission and identity of the Filipino church…[are] manifested in its love of God and country — *Pro Deo et Patria*."[136] This love of country finds expression in religio-patriotic ways: in the canonization of nationalist martyrs, in the white, blue and red vestments of clergy, in the presence of the Filipino flag in sanctuaries, and in the singing of nationalist hymns during liturgies.

The PIC's nationalist spirit might best be evidenced in its portrayal of Mary, the mother of Jesus, as Our Lady of Balintawak. In 1896, Andrés Bonifacio declared the Philippine Revolution in Balintawak, sharing his now-famous "Cry of Balintawak." Aglípay's "Novena in Honor of Our Lady of Balintawak" shares the story: When Bonifacio and other members of the Katipunan were staying in Balintawak, one Katipunero dreamed that he saw Mary dressed like a Filipina farmer, in the white, blue and red colors of what would become the national flag. She cried, "Liberty! Liberty!" as she led by the hand a boy dressed as a Katipunan guerilla. Hearing of this vision, Bonifacio and his followers chose to remain in Balintawak and not to return to Manila, where the Spanish military raided the *Manila Daily* and captured a number of Katipuneros. Filipino writer and Katipunan co-founder Aurelio Tolentino later wrote that this dream kept Bonifacio safe from capture and inspired the first Katipunan soldiers to wear red trousers in her honor. More importantly, the message was clear: Our Lady of Balintawak would guide and protect her Filipino sons and daughters in their quest for freedom and independence!

Historians Reynaldo C. Ileto and Francis Gealogo note how the image of Our Lady of Balintawak is a Filipino inculturation of the Roman Catholic faith received from Spanish missionaries. The original figurine at María Clara Christ Church in Santa Cruz, Manila, contains an inscription that might be translated, "Father, may the joyful day of our independence be born and shine forth!" The image quickly became "one of the most popular figures of Aglipayan iconography and religious portraiture prominently displayed in a number of pre-war, pre-concordat Aglipayan churches across the archipelago."[137]

Supreme Bishop Aglípay noted that Our Lady of Balintawak

> reminds you constantly of your sacred and inescapable duty to make every effort possible to obtain our longed-for independence; and she is the sacred image of our Country. The voice of the people will constantly resound from our pulpits, reminding you of the great teachings of Rizal, Mabini, Bonifacio and other Filipinos, and these teachings of our greatest compatriots will form the special seal of our National Church.[138]

In his novena in her honor, Supreme Bishop Aglípay noted that Our Lady of Balintawak symbolized the Motherland and that the child symbolized the Filipino people yearning for independence. He wrote:

> For the Country is the only mother that can truly be called Virgin, Virgin as it is of all lust. The Katipunero child represents the People, eager for their liberty, and their spokesmen, prophets and evangelists are the great Filipino teachers: Rizal, Mabini, Bonifacio, and our other countrymen whose modern sapient teachings will form the best national Gospel.[139]

Interestingly, Supreme Bishop Aglípay wove into his novena the nationalist writings of several Filipino heroes, including the Decalogue of Mabini, the Kartilya of the Katipunan, and excerpts from Rizal's letters and essays.

Due to its widespread appeal as a nationalistic church, the PIC experienced rapid growth. On August 31, 1904, in its "Facts in Few Lines" section, the *Iowa City Daily Press* noted that "Gregorio Aglípay claims to have 3,000,000 followers in his independent church movement in the Philippines."[140]

A Rational Faith

During the initial years of the PIC, Isabelo de los Reyes, Sr. created a distinct doctrine, liturgy, and organization for the Aglipayan church. Though never a Mason, he drew inspiration from Miguel Morayta, the Grand Master of the Spanish Orient Lodge of Freemasonry in Madrid, and he borrowed concepts of theology and worship from the Masonic Code. Supreme Bishop Aglípay later joined the Freemasons in 1918. As a result, they sometimes expressed their faith in ways that differed from traditional Roman Catholic theology.

According to initial documents created by de los Reyes and later approved by Supreme Bishop Aglípay,

> The church was founded principally to worship the one true God and to liberate the human conscience from "all scientific error, exaggeration and scruple." They rejected the doctrine of the Trinity as well as the possibility of miracles, including those mentioned in the New Testament. A new version of the Gospel was produced based exclusively on that of Saint Mark; the other evangelists were considered apocryphal. In this version, angels, devils, miracles, and other manifestations of the supernatural do not exist. Revelation and prophecy are denied.[141]

Because his priests served people deeply embedded in the Roman Catholic culture, though, Supreme Bishop Aglípay struggled to help them bring their people to a new expression of their Catholic faith. In 1903, Methodist Bishop Homer Stuntz explained it this way:

> There are inherent weaknesses in the new movement which Aglipay himself sees, but declares himself powerless to remedy. These are the sacerdotalism, saint worship, Mariolatry, and superstition of orthodox Romanism, all of which come into the new organization unchanged.[142]

Now free from the dogmatic theology of the Roman church, Supreme Bishop Aglípay espoused a progressive, rationalist faith. Jesuit Fathers Pedro de Achútegui and Miguel Bernad referred to his 1904 Lenten series as examples of "the most rationalistic religion

60

based on the Bible."[143] Aglípay's 1905 catechism[144] and 1926 Novenary of the Motherland also manifested this rational faith.[145] Similarly, de los Reyes published a 1906 divine office containing a "unified gospel of our Lord Jesus Christ, carefully purged of heresy and other interpolations"—which became known as the "Filipino gospel."[146]

Quite different from traditional Catholic creeds,

> The Aglipayan creed states that God is a universal and intelligent force, the principle of all life and movement. Satisfaction of human needs is achieved through work, rather than prayer. All reward and punishment for virtuous or evil behavior occur in this life. The origin of the universe is explained. The origin of the universe is explained as development and not creation, because matter has no beginning.[147]

Unlike traditional dialectics, Aglípay's catechism begins with the question: "Upon possessing the use of reason, what is the first thing the human person should ask him/herself?"[148] Perhaps nowhere, though, is the rational faith of the Aglipayan church more evident than in its illumination of the errors of "Romanist theologians" with respect to the traditional doctrine of the Trinity. In an extended treatment, Aglípay reasoned:

> How many gods are there? Only one in and for all people (Dt. 6:1 Is. 46:9, 1Cor 8:6), with different names; but the same God.
>
> Do you believe it rational that non-Christian people are condemned solely for not believing in Christ? That is absolutely absurd, because God—who even for the evil "is slow to anger and great in mercy and truth" (Ps. 86:15)—will undoubtedly not punish the innocent, since they are not to blame for not knowing Christ as we understand him. Nor is it wise to judge that the Divinity gave the true God to some people and a false God to others. That which is rational and established is the belief that the God of different people is the same, but worshiped with different names and in different ways, perhaps because harmony and beauty demand variety.
>
> Is it true that there exist three persons and only one God? That is also an enormous absurdity, since it is not possible

for three persons to exist without having three essences. Nor is it possible for a single essence to possess more than a single person. In the same way, it would be a frightening aberration to maintain that the Spirit of the Father is distinct from the Holy Spirit and the Spirit of Jesus, since having three distinct spirits, it would be necessary to confess three Gods.

Where, then, have some Christians gotten the idea that the Father, the Son and the Holy Spirit are three persons but one, true God? This is reminiscent of the ancient polytheism of barbaric people. In all the Bible, there is no talk of more than one God. It was an error of thinking and more than an error; it was a capricious interpretation of the sacred Scriptures which only aimed to collate divine unity with the error of religious polytheism, which was believed long before our scriptures, as was demonstrated in detail in our official publication, *The Philippine Independent Church.*

How do Romanist theologians explain the Most Holy Trinity? They say that in the beginning God the Father existed and only knowing himself, he engendered the Son; then these two divine persons loved one another, and, by their act of love, they engendered the Holy Spirit. This explanation is not found in the Bible, nor is it even half rational. This would mean that the Word and the Holy Spirit are engendered, which means that they are not eternal.

[Some might respond,] How dare you say that it's not even half rational? We don't say this ourselves, but all wise, modern persons who feel affect and admiration for Christianity, but who possess sufficient wisdom to think without prejudices and who have sufficient character to not allow themselves to be guided by fanatics who believe what they hear, even if it's an enormous absurdity.

[Some might ask,] So, the Philippine Independent Church doesn't believe in the Most Holy Trinity? Yes, she believes in it, but, since she is a civilized Church and a daughter of the 20th century, she believes it according to modernist, Christian criteria, which do not compromise with the polytheism that is improper for civilized people to pride themselves in possessing. It would be polytheism to believe in the trinity of persons, as we have demonstrated in an irrefutable way.[149]

To support his thesis on the absurdity of the Trinity, Supreme Bishop Aglípay continued with a detailed, catechetical explanation of how the Father, Son and Spirit manifest as a single God.

While denying the Trinity, many early Aglipayans recognized the divinity of Christ. In 1919, however, various voices in the Aglipayan church began to emphasize science as the source of all religious truth, illuminate the errors in Jesus' teachings, and cast a shadow on the Ten Commandments as pure myth. As a result, the revised plan for PIC studies encouraged "discarding...what is said about Christ's divinity, a doctrine which we accepted in the beginning only out of compulsion."[150]

The rationalist thought of the Aglipayan Church is also evident in subsequent chapters of the catechism. "Creation According to the Bible and Geology" expounds as much science as theology and concludes that geology "is founded on more solid and scientific bases than the computations made through generations of patriarchs."[151] "The Creation of Humankind Biblically-interpreted through the Natural Sciences" warns that the Bible should not be literally interpreted, as if a woman were created from the rib of a man, it and attempts to harmonize Charles Darwin's theory of evolution—"the greatest scientific glory of the 19th century"[152]—with the Bible. Constant reference is made to the "indisputable authority of wise natural scientists, upon whom we base our doctrines."[153] "Original sin is dismissed as an "enormous absurdity."[154] The Aglipayan catechism deviates from Roman Catholic catechisms in many ways, including "the criteria of the Philippine Independent Church that all religions are good and that the sacred books of all people are equally respectable."[155] It states,

> All religions, upon pretending to discover the profundities of this world, fall into ridiculous affirmations which have no foundation but absurd, mythological legends or capricious cavilocities. We therefore opine that, for the seriousness of our Religion, it is of great convenience to speak as little as possible about angels and demons. Undoubtedly, all the visions that simple people believe

they have about them are hallucinations of disequilibrated fantasies.[156]

The Philippine Independent Church thus attempted to balance seeming opposites—including modern science and an ancient faith. The Aglipayan church's motto expressed this tension: "Bible and Science, Love and Liberty." In contrast with the Roman church, the Aglipayan church did not discourage adherents from reading scriptures or learning about their world; instead, it encouraged the study of natural sciences, nuanced readings of scripture, and an exploration of the commonalities between Christianity and other spiritual traditions.

In contrast with the fortress mentality of the Tridentine Roman church, Supreme Bishop Aglípay modeled an ecumenical spirit, opening doors for future cooperation between the Philippine Independent Church and other denominations. He shared a particular fondness for Unitarianism. Together with Bishops Santiago Fonacier and Isabelo de los Reyes, Jr., Supreme Bishop Aglípay traveled to Boston for the annual convention of the Unitarian Association in March 1931. The convention passed resolutions in support of Philippine independence, admitted the PIC to the International Association of Liberal Christianity, and channeled significant financial support to the church.[157] While in the United States, the three prelates were feted by Unitarians throughout the nation, and Supreme Bishop Aglípay received an honorary degree from Meadville Theological School, a Unitarian seminary in Chicago. In 1939, Supreme Bishop Aglípay reciprocated by naming Dr. Louis C. Cornish of the American Unitarian Association an Honorary President of the PIC and by inviting him to serve as a witness at his wedding. These Unitarian encounters led Supreme Bishop Aglípay to revise his personal theology, reject belief in the Trinity, and align the PIC with the American Unitarian Association. As a result, the prayers and hymns of the early Aglipayan church were often an inconsistent mix of Unitarian and Trinitarian belief.

In a letter dated August 12, 1947, Bishop Norman Binsted of the Episcopal Church explained the possible roots of Aglipayan Unitarianism:

I believe the swing towards Unitarianism was a reaction due to the impact of rationalism on minds trained only in medieval obscurantism—and because Unitarians in America were quick to offer friendship and cooperation. I am told, and I believe it to be true, that never at any time did more than five percent of the people of the Church depart from the Trinitarian faith in which they had been grounded in their youth in the Roman Catholic Church. In recent years, the clergy and people have consistently adhered to the Trinitarian position (three of their churches are dedicated to the Holy Trinity). However, due to Dr. Aglípay's publications, the stigma of Unitarianism has stuck.[158]

Despite the close relationship between Supreme Bishop Aglípay and Dr. Cornish of the American Unitarian Association, their organizations were connected at the level of national leadership, but the majority of Aglipayan clergy and laity remained Trinitarian. Many Aglipayans even rejected Aglípay's Unitarian theology. A divide soon surfaced between the rationalist, Unitarian views of the shepherd and the more traditional views of many of his sheep, with Aglípay placing his priests who ministered to traditional, Trinitarian Catholics at risk of losing their congregants and income as a result of such innovations to the Catholic faith.

Fractures occurred. Ángel Flor Mata called his spin-off the *Iglesia Filipina Reformada* (Philippine Reformed Church), and, in 1924, Ciriaco de las Llagas founded the *Iglesia Filipina Evangélica Independiente* (Independent Philippine Evangelical Church). In 1928, an open battle erupted in the PIC over the divinity of Christ and other traditional dogmas, leading Servando Castro, the Aglipayan bishop of Ilocos, and five other founding members of the Aglipayan movement to publicly protest the Unitarian doctrine that de los Reyes and Aglípay had introduced without the approval of the Supreme Council of Bishops. They argued that "the rank-and-file Aglipayans held to the traditional teachings, that immutability is a characteristic quality of religious truths, and further that the new doctrines were contrary to the faith that the leaders of the Aglipayan church publicly swore to preserve."[159]

Ten years later, in April 1939, Bishop Isabelo de los Reyes, Jr., the son of PIC founder Isabelo de los Reyes, Sr., broke from the PIC, forming a Trinitarian faction.

The Presidential Candidate

1935

A former congressman, Supreme Bishop Aglípay knew the power and influence that comes from organizing people and resources. Shortly after its founding, he spurred his new church to organize the Republican party, which won seats in the first Philippine Assembly of 1907, and which later produced many senators, representatives, governors and mayors.[160]

Supreme Bishop Aglípay led a sizeable church, with some 1,413,506[161] or 1,417,448[162] followers listed in the 1918 Philippine census. A third of the population of Manila self-identified as Aglipayan at that time.[163] By the 1939 census, the number of Aglipayans had climbed to 1,573,608,[164] though this number represented a decrease in the percentage of Christians, from 15.2% of Christians who self-identified as Aglipayan in 1918, to 10.8% of whom did so in 1939. As their shepherd, Supreme Bishop Aglípay involved himself in the political struggles of the people, often aligning himself with nationalist and radical political parties, including the socialist and communist parties. Consistent with his desire to empower people, he supported peasant uprisings and political resistance to American imperialism.

After the U.S. Congress' Tydings-McDuffie Act of 1934, which provided a roadmap to Philippine independence by 1945, elections were scheduled for a president of the ten-year commonwealth that would result from that legislation. In 1935, at age 75 and with little money, Supreme Bishop Aglípay ran as a Republican candidate for the presidency, the third of three candidates to enter the race. Supported by an alliance of political parties known as the Coalition of the Oppressed Masses, Supreme Bishop Aglípay ran with vice presidential candidate Norberto Nabong. Their opponents were Nationalist party candidate General Emilio Aguinaldo and the eventual victor, Manuel Luis Quezón y Molina, who enjoyed the support of both the Nationalist-Democratic party and the similarly-named Pro-independence Nationalist Democratic Party. In contrast to Quezón, Aguinaldo and Aglípay were perceived as "two individuals who have heretofore engaged little in politics, but who have loyal followings."[165] Aglípay's church at the time was estimated to possess more than 10% of the Philippine population.[166] According to one U.S. newspaper, "Aglípay [had] been discussed frequently as a possible vice presidential candidate on Aguinaldo's ticket, and the announcement that he would seek the presidency was unexpected."[167] An article in the *San Antonio Express* stated that

> General Aguinaldo, who led the insurrection against the United States in 1899-1901, and Bishop Aglipay, head of the Independent Catholic Church of the Philippines, attacked Quezon in the campaign and advocated a shorter road to complete independence than the 10-year transition period provided in the Tydings-McDuffie act of Congress."[168]

Three months earlier, in June, the newspaper announced:

> The third (so far) candidate is Gregorio Aglipay, who heads the Independent Catholic Church of the Philippines. The Associated Press reports that he has not yet definitely formulated his platform, but his main purpose is to "beat Quezon," and a "Republican party" is being formed to support him.[169]

The following month, the newspaper provided a fuller picture of the supreme bishop:

> Gregorio Aglipay, who founded the Independent Philippine Church 30 years ago, is a candidate for the presidency of the commonwealth which will be created next November. He has been a picturesque figure since 1897, when he joined General Emilio Aguinaldo in an uprising against the Spanish colonial government at Manila....Aglipay was a chaplain, with colonel's grade, early in the second insurrection. He surrendered in 1901 and organized a native church, with himself as bishop. Aglipay is from the Ilocano group, that inhabits Northwest Luzon. Aguinaldo and Senator Manuel L. Quezon, his opponents, are Tagalogs, whose tongue is different; but all speak Spanish fluently and Quezon also speaks English. Aglipay announces that he is "out to beat Quezon," but the latter is supported by the dominant Nationalist party, that he has led for many years past. Aglipay may run ahead of Aguinaldo, who remained aloof from public life after President Theodore Roosevelt ordered his release, as a

war-prisoner, in July, 1902. Neither is likely to defeat Quezon.[170]

By the end of filing in August, cries of fraud surfaced. The *Oakland Tribune* reported:

> Nominations closed amid charges of planned fraud in the presidential election. The charges were made by Bishop Gregorio Aglipay of the Philippine Independent Catholic Church, presidential nominee of the Extremist Republican party, who advocated violence to prevent fraud. He asserted officials planned to abet frauds to ensure election of Senate President Manuel Quezon, nominee of the islands' two major parties.[171]

After the election, one U.S. newspaper reported that Aguinaldo and Aglípay, who were regarded as dark horses,[172] "were virtually snowed under."[173] The vote count reported by the Associated Press was 498,236 votes for Quezón, 152,963 for Aguinaldo, and 58,976 for Aglípay.[174] A recent typhoon in the Luzon province dampened voter turnout there, and Aguinaldo and Aglípay largely appealed to the same base, which was largely excluded from the election, since only literate, land-owning men were allowed to vote. One U.S. newspaper shared the opinion of an anonymous American official who claimed it was "an election shot through with frauds,"[175] while another expressed the post-election impossibility of a presidency by Aguinaldo or Aglípay, since the former desired independence from the U.S. in three to five years, and "Bishop Gregorio Aglipay was another impossibility, because he organized an INDEPENDENT church as the nucleus of a political party."[176] Another U.S. news report summarized the election results: "Bishop Aglipay, the Extremist Republican candidate…trailed Aguinaldo at the polls and probably will devote himself to church duties hereafter."[177]

The Roman Catholic editors of the *San Antonio Express* never missed an opportunity to snipe at Aglípay. The paper, which previously called Aglípay "a stormy petrel [seabird] in Philippine affairs for many years past,"[178] now shared an alarmist story by the Associated Press, titled, "Church War in Philippines Seen."[179] The article reported the Roman Catholic bishop of Cagayan's concern over an imminent clash between Roman Catholics and members of the Philippine Independent Church, who apparently built a chapel on land belonging to a public school. The biases of the patriotic, Roman Catholic author are evident:

> The colorful Aglipay headed the extremist republican party and ran unsuccessfully for commonwealth president last September. A Communist was his running mate. He ran far behind Coalitionist Manuel Quezon, who was elected, and Emilio Aguinaldo, old-time insurrecto. Aglipay originally was a Roman Catholic priest but was excommunicated when he assailed the pope and the Spanish friars. He then established a native church claiming a membership of 1,500,000 and 2,000,000. As a soldier, he fought with Aguinaldo against Spain and later against the United States.[180]

In 1938, Supreme Bishop Aglípay was numbered among "anti-administration Filipino leaders" who endorsed a resolution by U.S. Congressman Thomas O'Malley, a Democrat of Wisconsin, for the immediate independence of the Philippines. One news report stated that the "anti-administrationists headed by Bishop Gregorio Aglipay of the Popular Front, former presidential candidate, radioed…'We earnestly support your resolution stressing the fact our mass demands for immediate independence.'"[181]

Father & Husband: An Example for Other Clergy

The other very significant event late in Supreme Bishop Aglípay's life was his marriage at age 78. Years prior, he entered into a relationship with Pilar Jamias, sister of Juan Jamias, who was ordained a priest by the captive Roman Catholic bishop José Hevia Campomanes on November 26, 1898.

Twenty-six years before their marriage, on February 24, 1913, Gregorio and Carmen gave birth to a daughter, Liwliwa (Consuelo, in Spanish), who later served as Philippine secretary of the Rationalist Society of London and translated Supreme Bishop Aglípay's correspondence to English for contacts abroad. Supreme Bishop Aglípay referred to her as "my hope and partner in my struggles for the ideals of justice and humanity."[182] On February 17, 1938, Liwliwa died one week before her 25th birthday and was buried in the Pasay Cemetery in Manila.

On March 12, 1939, in the twilight of his life and in accord with Liwliwa's dying wish,[183] Supreme Bishop Aglípay married Liwliwa's mother, 64-year-old Pilar. Bishop Fernando Buyser officiated the wedding at the Aglipayan church in Tondo, Manila, and the couple's American, Unitarian friends, Dr. Louis and Frances Cornish, served as witnesses. Supreme Bishop Aglípay explained that he felt compelled to marry "in order to set an example for his followers, particularly the priests, that they could get married in conformity with the liberal teachings of his church."[184] Pilar survived her husband and ran for Vice President of the Philippines the next year, in 1941.[185]

The Passing of the First Supreme Bishop

1940

Supreme Bishop Aglípay led the Philippine Independent Church for 38 years, until a stroke left him motionless. On August 30, 1940, Bishop Santiago Fonacier visited Supreme Bishop Aglípay, who struggled to communicate his last words: *"Gracias que..."* ("Thank you for...").

On September 1, Supreme Bishop Gregorio Aglípay died at the age of 80. The Filipino people celebrated his life and legacy with an impressive funeral befitting the legendary guerrilla fighter and patriot, attended by the President of the Commonwealth, his Cabinet, and many of the highest state officials. At the time, the mourning Philippine President, Manuel Quezón, said:

> I have learned with profound sorrow of the death of Monsignor Aglipay. His services to the country during the revolution were of inestimable value and marked him as a Filipino patriot of the first rank. In this respect, our people should forever be grateful to him. I became his personal friend since 1907 and have felt great affection for him throughout these years, even during the presidential campaign when we were political opponents.[186]

In an address entitled, "Bishop Aglipay: the Man and Patriot," Ilocos Norte Governor Roque B. Ablán said:

> No one can deny that whether on the bloody battlefields, in the sacred prescient of his cathedral, and in the routine of his everyday life, he had one possessing obsession and that was to serve his country, that the Filipino nation might live, and that the Filipino people merit the respect that is its due. Bishop Aglipay received for heritage a duty, and that duty he discharged to the full measure of his ability. That duty was to collaborate with others to form a heterogeneous mass into a compact whole to be known as the Filipino nation....Whether fighting in the battlefields, in his Church, or in politics, nobody can deny his courage, his tenacity, and his sincerity of purpose.[187]

The remains of Supreme Bishop Aglípay were laid to rest at the Aglipayan Shrine in Batac, Ilocos Norte.

One U.S. newspaper reported that, at the time of his death, Aglípay's church consisted of 5,000 churches with a membership of four or five million people — a number that was vastly greater than the numbers of followers reported during Aglípay's presidential campaign five years earlier.[188]

Supreme Bishop Santiago Fonacier

1940-1946

Bishop Santiago Antonio Fonacier y Suguitan succeeded Aglípay as Supreme Bishop of the Philippine Independent Church. Born in Laoag, Ilocos Norte on May 21, 1885, he was one of 13 children of Dionisio Romero Fonacier and Feliciana Manuel. Part of the PIC since its founding, Santiago was ordained by age 18. He earned his bachelor degree from the *Escuela Docente* (Teaching School) of Laoag and taught for two years before founding and editing various Spanish periodicals, including *La Lucha* (*The Struggle*), which survived until 1941. Father Santiago reported for *La Democracia* (*Democracy*) and *El Grito del Pueblo* (*The Cry of the People*). He also translated a number of books into Ilocano, including Felice Guzzoni's *The Cardinal's Daughter*, José Rizal's *Noli Me Tangere* and *El Filibusterismo*, and Voltaire's *Candide* and *The Sage and the Atheist*.[189]

After nine years of priestly ministry, including time as a military chaplain, Father Santiago took a leave from active ministry, from 1912 to 1931. Like Supreme Bishop Aglípay, he served in elected office, initially as a representative of Ilocos Norte in the third Philippine Assembly from 1912 to 1916. In 1919, he was elected a senator in Ilocos Sur, and he served in that position for six years. He was elected to the Board of Regents of the University of the Philippines, as well as to the boards of the Institute of National Language, the National Textbook Board, and the Philippine Independence mission to the United States.

Father Santiago married Carmen Marcelina Amor Jamias y Ver, the niece of Juan Jamias, who was the brother-in-law of Supreme Bishop Aglípay. Together, the couple raised eight children.

Father Santiago was consecrated a bishop on January 12, 1933 at the Tondo Cathedral in Manila. On October 14, 1940, one month after Supreme Bishop Aglípay's passing, he was elected Supreme Bishop by the PIC General Assembly, and Bishop Isabelo de los Reyes, Jr. was elected General Secretary. Bishop Servando Castro of Ilocos, who previously protested the Unitarian bent of the Aglipayan church, withdrew his name from the election for Supreme Bishop on the condition that the Aglipayan church implement the 1902 Bacarra Formula, to steer the church back in the direction of a national catholic church with a Trinitarian faith, and away from its assumed identity as a liberal Christian church with a Unitarian faith.[190] Supreme Bishop Fonacier was installed on November 21, 1940, in a solemn ceremony attended by high government officials.

Within three months of Aglípay's passing, the Associated Press reported the following extended article outlining Fonacier's vision to grow the church and establish schools and colleges.

> Filipino desire for political independence today had its religious offshoot when Bishop Santiago Antonino Fonacier, newly elected "obispo maximo" of the Church of Aglipay, launched his campaign to convert Filipino Catholics and Protestants alike to the Philippine Independent Church.
>
> Bishop Fonacier succeeded Bishop Gregorio Aglipay as spiritual leader of the 2,000,000 Aglipayans.
>
> Aglipay was the founder of the organization, which broke from the Roman Catholic Church in 1902. Bishop Fonacier hopes to establish a purely nationalistic church "of the Filipinos." He advocates severing of all religious ties with other countries.
>
> "It is not for us to sleep on our laurels," he told the consistory of 42 Aglipayan priests and laymen after his election. "It is rather for us to be always active and alert, and to work, work, work. Let us work unceasingly, with enthusiasm and true faith, and let us not rest until we have attained the full realization of those solemn aims which obliged us to separate from the Church of Rome and to our own Philippine Independent Church, which is the true church of the Filipinos, for the Filipinos, and by the Filipinos."
>
> The first projected step in Bishop Fonacier's program will be establishment of religious schools and colleges, and especially of a central seminary in Manila, where the church would train young men from the islands.
>
> "What we need most," he declared, "are apostles and ministers of God, rich in faith, hope and charity, enthusiastic and active, because the lessons of history teach us that it is not the dogmas and doctrines of a church which

most contribute to its triumph, but apostles…armed with the faith that can transport mountains and divide the seas."

He admitted his plans for the future were in the nature of dreams.

Fonacier became the first head of the Church of Aglipay under its new "democratization" program. The church's consistory revoked an amendment approved in 1906 making the "obispo maximo" a life position. Fonacier will serve for three years, with the right to succeed himself once.

The "democratization" of the church, according to Bishop Fonacier, will be utilized "to reorganize and revitalize the office of "obispado maximo" [the Supreme Bishopric], so that everyone in the church, especially all bishops and priests, may be made to work for the church's advancement."

Bishop Fonacier became connected with the Philippine Independent Church since its founding. He was ordained at the age of 18 when the movement continued gaining momentum from Bishop Aglipay's charges that the Roman Catholic Church had become arbitrary if not corrupt in the Philippines.

He was "on leave" from the church from 1912 to 1931, during which time he became a political writer on the *Asamblea Filipina* [Philippine Assembly], a nationalistic Filipino-owned daily, which demanded immediate independence for the Philippines. He also served as a delegate from 1912 to 1916 to the third Philippine Assembly. He served as senator from 1919 to 1925, during which time he became a member of the University of the Philippines Board of Regents and a member of the second parliamentary mission to the United States in 1922 to lobby for independence.[191]

Supreme Bishop Fonacier is remembered for leading the PIC during the four-year occupation of the Philippines by the Japanese during World War II (1942-1945). While some 500 American Roman Catholic and Protestant missionaries were sent to an internment camp in Los Baños,[192] Supreme Bishop Fonacier chose to cooperate with

Japanese authorities and so allow his largely-Filipino clergy to continue their ministries.

During Supreme Bishop Fonacier's leadership of the church, on February 6, 1945, the Tondo cathedral was destroyed during the indiscriminate bombing of Manila by U.S. forces. The 2002 PIC History Committee recounts:

> During the Japanese occupation, church leaders fought for their convictions as they had done through the years. Good relations with Japanese authorities enabled the clergy to obtain passes and therefore mobility to serve the people. Japanese authorities, attempting to obtain cooperation of the Filipino people, however, befriended the church leadership. The political crisis constrained the hierarchy of the Church to cooperate with Japan. The *Obispo Máximo* and the General Secretary were made to broadcast favorable accounts of Japanese occupation of the Philippines as part of the Greater East Asia Co-Prosperity Sphere. However, a deviating opinion started to be articulated by the General Secretary, when he started proclaiming that true nationalism means unity of all Filipinos in defending their nation from all forms of foreign invasion.[193]

During the leadership of Supreme Bishop Fonacier, controversy divided the PIC. On September 2, 1945, the Supreme Council of Bishops appointed Bishop Alejandro Remollino as head of the Diocese of Cavite. Two weeks later, on September 18, 1945, Supreme Bishop Fonacier asked that Bishop Remollino await the Supreme Bishop's approval to assume leadership of the diocese. Remollino replied the next day that Former Supreme Bishop Aglípay had appointed him Bishop of Cavite and that, since the Supreme Council of Bishops now approved his appointment, he was "ready to defend [his] stand on the matter before the courts of justice."[194] Sparking a feud, Supreme Bishop Fonacier announced Bishop Remollino's transfer to the Diocese of Cebu.

On December 4, 1945, the Supreme Council of Bishops convened and charged Supreme Bishop Fonacier with failure to account for church funds, moving the church headquarters, and consecrating bishops in violation of the PIC constitution.

On January 21-22, 1946, the Supreme Council of Bishops removed Supreme Bishop Fonacier and elected his successor. A legal battle ensued, lasting nine years as it made its way to the Philippine Supreme Court in 1955. The lawsuit ended with Bishop Isabelo de los Reyes, Jr. being named the legitimate head of the Philippine Independent Church.

Former Supreme Bishop Fonacier and his supporters formed the Independent Church of Filipino Christians (ICFC), the "Filipinistas." In 2019, Dionito M. Cabillas enumerated more than ten ICFC communities still in existence.

The two churches diverged for nearly 20 years, until June 26, 1973, when they signed a memorandum of agreement. This opened the door for Former Supreme Bishop Fonacier to be welcomed back to the PIC and for the two churches to be reunited through a solemn mass of reconciliation at the national cathedral on March 24, 1974.

Three years later, on December 8, 1977, Bishop Fonacier died at the age of 92 in Pasay City. In 1985, he was honored with his likeness on a Philippine postage stamp.

Supreme Bishop Gerardo Bayaca

1946

After the leadership of Supreme Bishop Fonacier, Supreme Bishop Gerardo Bayaca y Medina led the church for fewer than eight months.

Born in Laoag, Ilocos Norte on September 23, 1893, Gerardo earned his bachelor of philosophy and theology from the Vigan Seminary and was ordained to the Roman Catholic priesthood on June 6, 1919. Father Gerardo incardinated into the PIC in October 1933. It is unclear when he was consecrated a bishop.

Amid the controversy over the Supreme Council of Bishops' removal of Supreme Bishop Fonacier, Bishop Bayaca was elected Supreme Bishop on January 22, 1946. He served in this capacity through September 1, 1946, when the factions within the PIC widened, resulting in the elections of two Supreme Bishops by two factions. Former Supreme Bishop Bayaca sided with Supreme Bishop Isabelo de los Reyes, Jr., and the two filed suit against rival Supreme Bishop Juan Jamias. While the case escalated to the Philippine Supreme Court, Former Supreme Bishop Bayaca received apostolic succession alongside Supreme Bishop de los Reyes on April 7, 1948.

Little is known of the last 25 years of Supreme Bishop Bayaca's life, leading up to his passing in December 1975 in Botolan, Zambales.

Supreme Bishop Isabelo de los Reyes, Jr.

1946-1971

After the brief leadership of Supreme Bishop Bayaca, Isabelo de los Reyes y López, Jr. assumed leadership of the church for 25 years.

Born on February 14, 1900 in Barcelona Spain to famed PIC fonder, Isabelo de los Reyes, Sr. and his wife, María Ángeles López Montero, Isabelo Junior was one of 27 children born to Isabelo Senior by age 51, a fact that circulated in many newspapers.[195]

Isabelo Junior was ordained to the priesthood on September 24, 1923 at María Clara Christ Church in Santa Cruz, Manila. Less than 16 months later, at age 24, he was consecrated to the episcopate in the same church on January 23, 1925.

As a young bishop in March 1931, de los Reyes traveled with Supreme Bishop Aglípay to Boston, where they attended the annual conference of the Unitarian Association and spoke at Unity Church in Montclair, New Jersey.[196]

After the death of Isabelo de los Reyes, Sr. in 1938, Bishop de los Reyes rejected the Unitarian views of his father and of Supreme Bishop Aglípay, exited the PIC, and formed an independent church with Trinitarian belief. Rumors suggested that Bishop de los Reyes' father renounced the PIC and returned to the Roman Catholic Church before dying, but his son vehemently denied such claims.[197]

On September 1, 1946, Bishop de los Reyes was elected Supreme Bishop by his faction of a now-divided church. Another faction, led by Former Supreme Bishop Fonacier, simultaneously elected Supreme Bishop Juan Jamias, the uncle of Fonacier's wife and the brother-in-law of Former Supreme Bishop Gregorio Aglípay. The two factions diverged over Aglípay's Unitarian theology, with the latter accepting it and de los Reyes rejecting it and seeking to enter into communion with other Christians of Trinitarian belief. Beginning in 1948, Supreme Bishop de los Reyes waged a legal battle with the Unitarian faction for the sole right to the name, possessions and properties of the PIC. The war waged for nearly 20 years later, until 1955. Father Apolonio Ranche writes,

> The struggle for leadership between Santiago Fonacier and Isabelo de los Reyes, Jr. after the Japanese Occupation proved costly and sapped the strength of the Church. The

majority of members followed or supported Isabelo de los Reyes, Jr., who eventually won the court struggle in 1955.[198]

Leading a challenged church, Supreme Bishop de los Reyes worked to strengthen the PIC's institutional life and theological position. On August 5, 1947, under Supreme Bishop de los Reyes' leadership, the Trinitarian faction of the PIC adopted a new constitution and canons, to replace the church's 1903 constitution. The Trinitarian PIC also adopted a Declaration of Faith and Articles of Religion, whose articulation opened the door to bridgebuilding with other churches. The opening paragraph of the Declaration of Faith reads:

> The object of the founding of the Philippine Independent Church principally responds to the imperative need to restore the worship of the one true God in all its splendor and the purity of his most holy Word which, under the reign of obscurantism, has been diluted and distorted in a most disheartening manner for any Christian of even moderate education.[199]

After the 1946 independence of the Philippines from U.S. control and the reconstruction of the nation after World War II, Supreme Bishop de los Reyes severed ties with the revolutionary nationalism, rationalism and socialism that characterized the church co-founded forty years earlier by his father and Supreme Bishop Aglípay. No longer a church of revolutionary struggle, the Aglipayan church now focused on "sentimental Philippinism" and the passionate pursuit of ecumenism.

Supreme Bishop de los Reyes organized laity at the national level. On June 18, 1956, the Supreme Council of Bishops approved the formation of the National Laymen's Commission, which elected its first president, Apolonio Pisig, on September 1. The primary purpose of the guild was the construction of a new national cathedral, consecrated 13 years later. On May 10-11, 1957, the first national convention for Trinitarian PIC women at St. Andrew's Theological Seminary elected Ella Cabreza as its first president of the Women's Auxiliary of the Philippine Independent Church. In 1960, Raymundo Beltrán, a young attorney, organized a regional youth movement that was later recognized as a national youth movement in 1969.

In 1957, the General Assembly of the Trinitarian PIC amended the 1947 Constitution to extend the term of the Supreme Bishop, from two years, to four years. Four years later, in 1961, the General Assembly approved a new PIC missal and ritual. These liturgical revisions suppressed the church's previous nationalism and opened the door to greater international and interdenominational relations. Notably, the preface was modified, replacing the traditional petition for independence, freedom and abundant life with a prayer for the maintenance of independence already received.

Under the leadership of Supreme Bishop de los Reyes, the church engaged in building a new national cathedral. After the previous PIC cathedral was destroyed by indiscriminate bombing by U.S. forces in 1945, the heirs of the donor who gave the land for the former cathedral to Aglípay — without deed — reclaimed the lot. The PIC was left without a cathedral for over 20 years. Internal struggles diverted the attention of national leadership, causing the Trinitarian faction of the PIC to locate its national center of worship at María Clara Christ Church in Santa Cruz, Manila. That church, built in 1923, honored Supreme Bishop de los Reyes' mother, María Ángeles "Geliños" López Montero.

In May 1960, on the occasion of the centennial of former Supreme Bishop Gregorio Aglípay's birth, Supreme Bishop de los Reyes launched a nationwide fundraising campaign for a new cathedral on a lot later donated to the PIC in 1966 by the American Episcopal Church. He later noted that "in the National Cathedral, built with *centavos, pesetas* and *pesos* of the countless hundreds of thousands, we will serve our Lord Jesus Christ by serving and loving his Children, even to the humblest."[200] On December 18, 1964, Supreme Bishop de los Reyes celebrated the groundbreaking and laid the cornerstone of the cathedral, which was named in honor of the Holy Infant Jesus, the patron saint of the first national cathedral that was destroyed in Tondo. The Supreme Council of Bishops rejected the first design for the cathedral, and the final design was created by architect Carlos D. Arguelles, the designer of several notable buildings in and around Manila.

The 1960 census of the Philippines indicated a precipitous decline in the percentage of Aglipayans, who decreased from 10.8% of the Christian population in 1939, to 5.6% of the Christian population in 1960.[201] Under Supreme Bishop de los Reyes' administration, the Aglipayan share of Christian adherents continued to decline, to 4.2%

of the Christian population of the Philippines in 1970.[202] In 1964, de Achútegui and Bernad delved into the 1960 census data, enumerated 13 factions of the Aglipayan church, and contrasted PIC membership claims (e.g., "well over three million baptized members") with census data (viz., 1,414,431 self-reporting adherents).[203] They shared, for instance, the following discrepancies for nine cities alone between 1960 census data and the numbers contained in the 1961 PIC Directory:

City	1960 Census	1961 PIC Directory	Discrepancy
Cebu City	340	16,000	15,600
Davao City	570	6,500	5,930
Cagayan de Oro	8,685	34,400	25,715
Lucena City	160	2,100	1,940
Ballesteros (Cagayan)	7,841	21,500	13,659
Candijay (Bohol)	1,904	19,500	1,596
Tangub (Misamis Occ.)	808	9,000	8,192
Sariaya (Quezon)	939	4,200	3,261
San José (Samar)	2,442	11,000	8,558
Total	23,689	124,200	100,511

While the 1960 census enumerated 1,414,431 Aglipayans, Supreme Bishop de los Reyes suggested a membership of "approximately two million baptized persons."[204] Reasons may exist for such discrepancies, including the enthusiasm of those estimating and the fact that many Roman Catholics seek sacraments from Independent Catholic churches due to the excessive requirements and substantial sacramental fees asked of them by Roman Catholic parishes. Such persons are included in the sacramental records of Aglipayan churches, even though many self-identify neither as Aglipayans nor as members of the Independent Catholic parishes from which they receive their sacraments.

On May 8, 1969, the 109th anniversary of Former Supreme Bishop Gregorio Aglípay, thousands gathered to celebrate the inauguration of the cathedral, and all major newspapers editorialized the event.[205] The 2002 PIC History Committee wrote of the cathedral:

> In pursuit of the *Pro Deo et Patria* mission of the *Iglesia Filipina Independiente,* [the National Cathedral] remained a steadfast companion of the Filipino people in the pilgrimage towards the Kingdom of God. Its pulpit echoes

the prophetic voice of the *Iglesia Filipina Independiente* for justice and peace. In its altar is offered the struggle of the poor, deprived, and oppressed. It opens its doors to shelter the people from persecution as they assert their God-given rights to abundant life. In many times, present and past, the National Cathedral offered itself as a sanctuary to the marginalized sectors, in asserting their democratic rights amidst exploitation and oppression.[206]

Elected in 1946, Supreme Bishop de los Reyes was re-elected in 1949, 1951, 1953, 1957, 1961, 1965 and 1969. He served as Supreme Bishop through his death in Manila on October 10, 1971.

Aglipayans before the Philippine Supreme Court

In 1946, the two factions of the PIC immediately engaged in a legal battle for right to the church's property and funds. Both Supreme Bishop Isabelo de los Reyes, Jr. and Former Supreme Bishop Gerardo Bayaca appeared in a Manila court of first instance in 1948, where Judge Conrado Barrios ruled in favor of the defendant, Supreme Bishop Juan Jamias, naming him the "actual and legitimate supreme bishop of the church."[207] Judge Barrios based his ruling on the opinion that Supreme Bishop de los Reyes and Former Supreme Bishop Bayaca "are no longer members of the Aglipayan Church, as they have adjured the doctrine of this church by embracing that of the Protestant Episcopal Church of the United States"[208] For some years, it seemed that Supreme Bishop de los Reyes' plan to bring legitimacy to his church through the securing of apostolic succession had backfired.

On May 20, 1950, Judge Félix Martínez reversed the earlier decision and declared Supreme Bishop Isabelo de los Reyes, Jr. as the sole and legitimate bishop of the PIC, ordering Former Supreme Bishop Fonacier to surrender all church properties and funds.

The legal battle lasted nine years, as it made its way to the Philippine Supreme Court. On January 28, 1955, in the case of *Santiago A. Fonacier v. Court of Appeals and Isabelo de los Reyes, Jr.*, Supreme Bishop de los Reyes, Jr. was named the legitimate head of the Philippine Independent Church. Former Supreme Bishop Fonacier seceded from the PIC and formed the Independent Church of Filipino Christians (ICFC), and the two churches remained separate for nearly 20 years.

After the passing of Supreme Bishop de los Reyes in October 1971, Former Supreme Bishop Fonacier resumed dialogue with the PIC. On June 26, 1973, the two churches signed a memorandum of agreement that opened the door for Former Supreme Bishop Fonacier to be welcomed back to the PIC. The two churches reunited during a solemn mass of reconciliation at the national cathedral on March 24, 1974.

Securing Apostolic Succession

Now remembered as the "Father of Ecumenism in the Philippines," Supreme Bishop Isabelo de los Reyes, Jr. strengthened the position of the Trinitarian faction of the PIC during years of internal division, by forging concordat relations with various churches, including the Protestant Episcopal Church of the United States (PECUSA) and the Anglican Communion. He also enrolled his church—using the disputed name "Philippine Independent Church"—in the National Council of Churches in the Philippines, the Christian Conference in Asia, and the World Council of Churches.

In the words of one Roman Catholic apologist, Supreme Bishop de los Reyes sought to correct the "wistful realization that his church, founded 44 years ago by Gregorio Aglípay, an unfrocked priest, on a nationalistic basis, [was] essentially deficient" due to lack of valid Orders and Unitarian views of the Aglipayan church.[209] In 1946, resolved to secure apostolic succession from PECUSA, Supreme Bishop de los Reyes began communicating with Philippine Episcopal Missionary Bishop Norman Binsted, who later noted that the Japanese occupation of the Philippines brought the two together in 1941. Supreme Bishop de los Reyes expressed a desire to bring the Aglipayan church's "two million adherents into organic relation with historic Christianity and enable the two Churches to work together in closest harmony."[210] Similarly, in a letter to Bishop Binsted dated August 19, 1946, Judge Buenaventura Ocampo of the Philippine Court of First Instance expressed his gratitude for the Episcopal Church's willingness to consider Supreme Bishop de los Reyes' request, for the sake of "the spiritual salvation of millions of people."[211]

In an October 29, 1946 letter to PECUSA Presiding Bishop Henry St. George Tucker, Bishop Binsted, using language similar to de los Reyes', noted that Former Supreme Bishop Aglípay was consecrated by fellow priests and leaned toward Unitarianism, and that Governor William Howard Taft was named an "honorary bishop" of the church, but that the Aglipayan church, now consisting of 20 bishops, 400 priests and 1.5 millions members—all accepting the Lambeth Quadrilateral—"is Trinitarian and desires to place itself in organic relation with historic Christianity."[212] Bishop Binsted also asked Presiding Bishop Tucker's advice on allowing the Aglipayan church to use the Book of Common Prayer and on sending PIC students to the Episcopal seminary.

On January 20, 1947, PECUSA Presiding Bishop Henry Knox Sherrill acknowledged receipt of Bishop Binsted's letter and suggested that the matter be referred to the PECUSA House of Bishops.[213] Five days later, Bishop Binsted replied, suggesting that the House of Bishops invite Supreme Bishop de los Reyes to its meeting in November.[214] On February 13, 1947, Presiding Bishop Sherrill questioned whether Supreme Bishop de los Reyes should be invited to the meeting of the House of Bishops, since denial of his request to enter into communion with PECUSA could lead to embarrassment.[215]

In a February 10, 1947 letter to Presiding Bishop Sherrill, Reverend Floyd W. Tomkins of the PECUSA Advisory Council on Ecclesiastical Relations also suggested caution, counseling that the PIC "submit evidence as to its official teaching in regard to faith and order" and noting that the Aglipayan church's request to use the Book of Common Prayer "sounds as if they had no prayer book of their own."[216] Tomkins recommended that discussion of the matter be postponed until after the Lambeth Conference of 1948.

In a letter dated February 27, 1947, Bishop Binsted pointed out to Presiding Bishop Sherrill the four deficiencies that Supreme Bishop de los Reyes wished to humbly address within the Aglipayan church:

1. The invalid consecration of its fonder and the invalid ordinations of all who were not ordained by the Roman Catholic Church,
2. The Unitarian beliefs of Aglípay, which caused the doctrinal position of the church to be questioned,
3. The hastily-framed and inadequate constitution and canons adopted by the early church, and
4. The church's lack of uniformity in worship, with "some of their Priests using a revised form of the Roman Missal, some using our Book of Common Prayer, and some a service of their own."[217]

Bishop Binsted met the previous day with Supreme Bishop de los Reyes, five Aglipayan bishops, two priests and one layman. He suggested that the Supreme Council of Bishops clearly state the doctrinal position of the church, revise its constitution and canons, and make a formal application to the PECUSA for the consecration of its bishops. He summarized:

> In brief, this is the situation: Here is a body of about 1,500,000 Christians, who, about fifty years ago, rebelled against the authority of the Pope and the domination of the Spanish priests. They desired to retain Catholic faith and order. Bishop Aglipay, the founder, sought episcopal consecration at the hands of the Old Catholic bishops, and made some overtures to [Philippine Episcopal Missionary Bishop Charles Brent]. However, because [Aglipay] was closely associated with the political independence movement, and was undoubtedly a political as well as a religious leader, and moreover, had come strongly under the influence of the radical theological thought of the times, the Old Catholic bishops and Bishop Brent withheld approval of the movement pending further developments. Then the Unitarian Church in the U.S.A., perhaps on the advice of the then-Governor-General William Howard Taft, offered assistance and cooperation. This Bishop Aglipay accepted, along with the theology of the church. However, I am authoritatively informed that no more than five percent of the people of the Philippine Independent Church at any time accepted this new theology. The great body of the Priests and people remained loyal to the Catholic faith and practice to which they had been accustomed....Those with whom I have conferred wish permission to authorize the Book of Common Prayer as the standard Book of Worship in their Church, and permission to send their theological students to our Seminary after it has been established in Manila.[218]

On March 1, 1947, Bishop Sherrill replied to Bishop Binsted, expressing his hope and caution that the Aglipayan church create a formal statement on its doctrine before approaching the Ecclesiastical Relations Committee.

In an address to the PIC General Assembly on August 4, 1947, Bishop Norman Binsted told Aglipayans:

> Your Church has had an honorable history. It has contended with persecution from without and difficulties within. It was born in a day when rationalism was at its

height and some of your leaders, as a reaction to the obscurantism to which they had been exposed, came strongly under its influence. Then too your Church came into being when great statesmen of these Islands were in rebellion against foreign oppression. It was inevitable that your early leaders should make common cause with such men. However, through all the stress and strain of political and intellectual revolution, it is evident that God held you very closely to Himself, and caused you to cherish the Faith once for all delivered to the Apostles.[219]

At that General Assembly, the Supreme Council of Bishops and General Assembly of the PIC approved "a solemn Declaration of Faith and the Articles of Religion whereby [its] Church officially proclaims its exalted faith in the Holy Trinity…[and] in the divinity of our Lord Jesus Christ."[220]

On August 9, 1947, Supreme Bishop de los Reyes, in a letter endorsed by Secretary General Manuel Aguilar, petitioned PECUSA Presiding Bishop Henry Sherrill for the gift of apostolic succession, saying,

> Not less than two millions of Filipinos very respectfully join me in this humble invitation to the Protestant Episcopal Church of America to bestow upon us the grace of Apostolic Succession to allow our Church to remove all objections to the validity of our sacred orders and the validity of our Sacraments, and to be recognized as a young sister Church by the Anglican Communion of Churches.[221]

During a meeting in Winstead-Salem, North Carolina, on November 4-7, 1947, the Episcopal House of Bishops authorized the consecration of de los Reyes and two other Aglipayan bishops.

The consecration of Supreme Bishop de los Reyes, Former Supreme Bishop Gerardo M. Bayaca of Tarlac and Zambalas, and Bishop Manuel N. Aguilar of Laguna took place on April 7, 1948, at the Episcopal Pro-cathedral of St. Luke in Binondo, Manila. The consecrators included Episcopal Bishops Norman Spencer Binsted of the Philippines (acting for the Episcopal Church's Presiding Bishop, Henry Knox Sherrill), Suffragan Bishop Robert Franklin Wilner of the Philippines, and Bishop Harry Scherbourne Kennedy of Honolulu.

Some 500 people attended the consecration, including Aglípay's widow and General Emilio Aguinaldo, "who led the revolutionary movement at the beginning of the century which gave impetus to the new church."[222] The *Honolulu Star-Bulletin* published a photo of the consecration, showing Bishops Wilner, Kennedy and Binsted laying hands on Supreme Bishop de los Reyes, with Bishop Aguilar to be consecrated next.[223] The Associated Press also published a photo of the three new bishops.[224] Together, the three prelates later consecrated 20 other bishops.

Ten years later, in August 1958, the PIC became an active member of the World Council of Churches. In 1961, it participated in the Third Assembly of the World Council of Churches in New Delhi, India, where Bishop Macario Ga was elected a member of the Central Committee for a term of seven years, following by a second term in 1968.

On May 8, 1960, the centennial of the birth of Supreme Bishop Gregorio Aglípay, the PIC Supreme Council of Bishops and General Assembly unanimously approved a proposal for the PIC to enter into a concordat with PECUSA.

In September 1961, the General Convention of the American Episcopal Church approved a concordat of full communion with the Philippine Independent Church. The 2002 PIC History Committee reprinted poetic words seemingly from that era:

> By such historic action, the American Church has laid down a bridge of recognition between the American and Filipino Churches that shall assuredly promote a healthy trade of spiritual riches between the Christians of America and the Philippines. Through this concordat, the Filipino Church has strengthen its roots and has been welcomed into the open road that leads towards the reservation of its own identity and independence, while simultaneously assuring for its clergy and laity a gradual increase of living contacts with the national churches of the Anglican Communion….We rejoice, beyond the power of words to express, at the termination of our half-century of isolation, and no longer feel ourselves the orphans of the Pacific. We pledge to carry on our revolt and prove worthy of the concordat, not in terms of all or nothing, but adopting the principle of moderation and love for truth that, in the

words of Albert Camus, is the main characteristic of all proper revolutions.[225]

When the concordat relation was approved in 1961, a Joint Council was created to concretize the relation between the two churches. This PIC-PECUSA Joint Council later formed a student work program at the University of the Philippines, which generated the University of the Philippines/Philippine Independent Church Student Association (UPPICSA). These efforts cultivated social consciousness through educational programs and revived a spirit of nationalism among church youth.

Possessing an intercommunion agreement with the Episcopal Church, Supreme Bishop de los Reyes was invited to speak at various PECUSA churches in the United States. Newspapers reported some of these events, including one at St. Andrew's Cathedral in Honolulu on September 10, 1961, [226] on his way to the general convention in Detroit of the Episcopal Church. During his stay of more than a month in the United States, he shared a presentation at St. Stephen's Episcopal Church in Elwood, Indiana on October 27, 1961. The local newspaper reported that he spoke "in a most engaging manner…of his life and the work of his church before and after World War II, the present struggle with communism in the islands, and the challenge which confronts the church today."[227]

After the concordat of full communion with PECUSA, the PIC established full communion with the following:

- Province of the West Indies (September 1, 1962)
- Church of the Province of Central Africa (November 12, 1962)
- Church of the Province of West Africa (1962)
- Church of the Province of East Africa (1962)
- Church of India, Pakistan, Burma and Ceylon (January 18, 1963) – the first-ever concordat between Asian churches
- Nippon Sei Ko Kai, the Anglican Church in Japan (March 15, 1963)
- Church of Ireland (May 1963)
- Lusitanian Church (October 9, 1963)
- Church of England (October 16, 1963) – a significant step for the PIC
- Episcopal Church in Scotland (December 5, 1963)

- Anglican Church of Canada (1963)
- Church of Uganda, Rwanda and Burundi (1963)
- Spanish Reformed Church (1963)
- Church of the Province of South Africa (February 17, 1964)
- Church of the Province of New Zealand (April 29, 1964)
- Union of Utrecht of Old Catholic Churches (1965)
- Episcopal Church of Brazil (1965)

On November 7, 1963, Supreme Bishop de los Reyes, Jr. was elected the first Chairman of the National Council of Churches in the Philippines, at its inaugural assembly and first general convention at the Episcopal Cathedral of St. Mary & St. John in Quezon City.

In April 1964, the PIC established contact with the Orthodox Churches of the East. At the invitation of Arthur Michael Ramsey, Archbishop of Canterbury, Supreme Bishop de los Reyes and Bishop Tito Pasco attended the first meeting of the wider Episcopal Fellowship.

Supreme Bishop de los Reyes' subsequent travels to the U.S. were documented in newspapers. In November 1964, he served as a guest preacher at St. Peter's Episcopal Church in St. Petersburg, Florida. The local paper described him as a married bishop with ten children and as leading a "catholic, reformed and autonomous" church of three million people.[228] He returned to the United States five years later and spoke at Christ Episcopal Church in Eureka, California on April 22, 1966.[229]

On February 25, 1966, Bishop John E. Hines, Presiding Bishop of the Episcopal Church in the United States (ECUSA) signed a 99-year lease with the PIC for four pesos, for a .86-acre lot on Taft Avenue in Manila, where the official residence of the missionary bishop of the Episcopal Church once stood. Under Supreme Bishop de los Reyes' leadership, the National Cathedral of the Holy Infant Jesus was constructed there, and the ECUSA later donated the land to the PIC in 1972.

On September 22, 1966, Supreme Bishop de los Reyes hosted a celebration of the fifth anniversary of the PIC-ECUSA concordat. On November 2, 1967, he ratified a concordat of full communion with the Church of the Province of East Africa.

In 1968, Bishop Solimán Ganno and Father Vic Esclamado represented the PIC at the Fourth Regional Assembly of the East Asia

Christian Conference (EACC, later renamed the Christian Conference in Asia in 1973).

As a result of the PIC's close relationship with several Protestant churches, it has often been described as a church that combines elements of Catholic and non-Catholic traditions. One writer recently described the PIC as "a nationalist church 'Catholic' in tradition but 'Protestant' in action."[230] He explained:

> They're "Catholic" on grounds that the church proclaimed schism from the Roman Catholic Church, and it's retained some Catholic celebrations and doctrines in their theology…[but] though it's "Catholic," it is independent from Roman Catholicism and the papal authority. "Protestant" in action due to its alliances, full communion and concordats with Protestant denominations, such as the Lutheran, Episcopal, Methodist, Anglicans, and Ecumenical Churches.[231]

Toward the end of the 1960s, with the construction of the national cathedral now complete, Supreme Bishop de los Reyes' attention was diverted by the young adults who were creating a national movement within the church. As a result, the PIC convened its first-ever National Youth Assembly in 1969, where the assembly turned militant, with youth condemning the semi-feudal and semi-colonial conditions of Philippine society and challenging the church to take a clear stand on the issue. The assembly gave birth to the National Youth Movement of the PIC and elected Carmencita Karagdag as its chairperson. Later signaling the desire of young people to reclaim the nationalist character and heritage of the PIC, the organization changed its name to its Filipino equivalent, the *Kilusang Pambansa ng Kabataan ng Iglesia Filipina Independiente* (National Youth Movement of the PIC). It also became increasingly progressive and militant, uniting young people and supporting them as they asserted their role in the church and criticized the complacency of church leaders in the late 1960s. As a result, the 2002 IFI History Committee judged that 1969 marked "the reawakening of the revolutionary nationalism and re-politicization of the *Iglesia Filipina Independiente*."[232]

Supreme Bishop Macario Ga

1971-1981

After Supreme Bishop de los Reyes' 25 years of service to the church, Supreme Bishop Macario Ga y Vilches led the PIC for the next ten years. Born in Buenavista, Guimaras on April 10, 1913, he graduated with his bachelor of pre-law in 1933 and was ordained to the diaconate on April 10, 1934—his 23rd birthday—at the Tondo Cathedral in Manila. Less than a month later, he was ordained to the priesthood on May 8, 1934.

Father Macario was consecrated to the episcopacy on January 22— though the year is uncertain. Supreme Bishop de los Reyes shared apostolic succession with Bishop Ga on September 1, 1948, in La Paz, Iloilo, after receiving it himself on April 7, 1948.

In 1961, Bishop Ga participated in the Third Assembly of the World Council of Churches in New Delhi, India, where he was elected a member of the Central Committee for a term of seven years. He was reelected to a second term at the Fourth Assembly in Uppsala, Sweden in 1968.

Bishop Ga was elected Supreme Bishop of the PIC in November 1971. He was re-elected in 1973 and 1977, serving as Supreme Bishop until 1981.

Before Bishop Ga's election as Supreme Bishop, Filipino youth of the KPK-IFI gathered during the "First Quarter Storm" of 1970, to join Filipino protests against Philippine President Ferdinand Marcos. On April 28 to May 1, 1972, during the administration of Supreme Bishop Ga, they gathered for their Second National Assembly, "PIC Youth Face the Challenges of the 1970s." The PIC History Committee relates:

> The assembly denounced and opposed the unholy trinity of imperialism, bureaucratic capitalism, and feudalism, and issued a direct challenge to the conservative, opportunists and reactionary elements of the church on its open collaboration with the ruling regime. The same demanded reforms in the church and the restoration of the genuine teachings and history of the church.[233]

In April 1976, the PIC convened a National Youth Consultation at St. Andrew's Theological Seminary. Seventy youth representatives from 30 dioceses adopted a constitution and bylaws and demanded concrete reforms in the PIC, including increased lay involvement and the democratization of the church, and a National Youth Office. They also secured youth representation in the national church, beginning with the National Consultative Assembly at that national cathedral on October 21-24, 1976. A result of the growing demand for greater participation of the laity in the governance and administration of the church, the Assembly approved a 1977 Constitution for the church and a statement on church mission.

Significantly, the 1977 Constitution departed from episcopal polity, only agreeing after 1995 to the terms "episcopally-led" and "synodically-governed." Dr. Valiant O. Dayagbil states that this new Constitution mangled the 1947 Constitution and Canons and "came into being full of infirmities, departing from the spirit of 1902."[234] It changed the PIC from a sole corporation to an aggregate corporation governed by councils at the parish, diocesan and national levels. This problem became evident in 1981 when Former Supreme Bishop Ga waged a legal battle against the PIC over the contested authenticity of certain provisions approved in 1977.

Supreme Bishop Ga led the PIC when President Ferdinand Marcos placed the Philippines under martial law on September 23, 1972. President Marcos self-identified as an Aglipayan for years until he converted to Roman Catholicism in order to marry his wife, Imelda. The Supreme Bishop, like other Catholic and Protestant leaders, felt forced to collaborate with Marcos' dictatorship. PIC clergy and laity decried the staunch support of Supreme Bishop Ga for the dictatorship, even as other Catholic and Protestant prelates became increasingly critical of Marcos' despotic leadership. The PIC History Committee writes:

> The generation of young clergy and progressive youth of the church registered their opposition to the perfidy of supporting the anti-muslim and anti-communism crusade and new society ideology of Marcos, rightfully seeing them as demonstrations of unveiling state fascism….[while] the hierarchy willingly made the church a cultural apparatus for the moral justification of the strongman's garnering of absolute political power. Eventually, the clergy, seriously disturbed by the hierarchy's politicking, started to openly criticize its unapprised gesture of condoning the

dictatorship. Irritations started to grow between the hierarchy and a number of bishops, and the progressive clergy and laity. The tension was increased when the latter mounted a criticism on the anomalous practices of some bishops and the hierarchy and with their crusade to clean up the church bureaucracy.[235]

The ensuing period saw a rise in militancy among grassroots clergy and youth who hoped to renew the national and democratic heritage of the PIC. The 2002 PIC History Committee summarized:

> The UPPICSA and the IFI were caught in the vortex of political unrest against the much-hated U.S.-Marcos dictatorship. The rising nationalist current and restlessness of the militant students and mentors swept the universities and colleges. Worker and peasant movements in the countryside have been mounting and intensifying. The revolutionary fervor has inevitably challenged the IFI to look back to its origin and define its present task amidst the escalating social upheavals.[236]

On May 9, 1977, the PIC General Assembly approved a constitution that radically changed the structures of the church and mandated the creation of the National Priests Organization. The formation of this organization exacerbated tensions between the conservative, pro-martial-law PIC hierarchy, which sought to unify the church in support of the dictator, and the progressive, young priests, who desired to recapture the revolutionary nationalism of the early Aglipayan church and were now labeled by the hierarchy as subversives. Many priests and PIC youth were surveilled by the military or arrested. Even Supreme Bishop Ga congratulated government officials in 1981 for arresting and imprisoning his own priest, Father Jeremías "Jerry" Aquino, for suspected revolutionary activities. Father Jerry later wrote from prison:

> The stirring spirit that gave birth to our Church is seen to be totally paled by time and circumstances, if we forever hold our peace before the unfolding drama of the whole Filipino people. The IFI has a place under the sun only if she can recapture once again that spirit of an outer-oriented movement—a movement that wholeheartedly embraces the aspirations of the poor who make up the vast majority

of our people. After all, she started with her twin sister, *La Unión Obrera Democrática*, the fortress of the Filipino workingman. And to state proudly, the "wretched of the earth" were her pristine company.[237]

Meanwhile, Supreme Bishop Ga focused on stabilizing the church's finances, purchasing church properties, and building bridges with other denominations. As a result of his support for the dictatorship, President and First Lady Ferdinand and Imelda Marcos were the principal funders of the PIC's national shrine in Batac, Ilocos Norte, which was inaugurated by Supreme Bishop Ga in September 1977.

Supreme Bishop Ga continued relations with the Episcopal Church, attending the installation of Bishop Edmond Lee Browning of Hawaii on August 1, 1976.[238] He also reconciled the Philippine Unitarian Church, which splintered from the PIC and was founded by Bishop Pedro Aglípay in 1955.

The 1977 General Assembly approved a new PIC constitution and canons, which encouraged greater governance by laity in the life of the church. The resulting education and stewardship programs strengthened the PIC. In 1980, the PIC opened two regional seminaries: Aglípay Central Theological Seminary in Urdaneta, Pangasinan and St. Paul Theological Seminary in La Paz, Iloilo (which later moved across the Iloilo Strait to the island of Guimaras).

On May 8, 1981, Supreme Bishop Ga expected to be reelected by the 232 bishops, priests and lay persons at the first General Assembly held under the new 1977 Constitution. To his surprise, clamor for change by PIC youth and the National Priests Organization led the General Assembly to elect Bishop Abdias de la Cruz y Rebantad to be his successor. Former Supreme Bishop Ga refused to concede and unsuccessfully petitioned that the Securities and Exchange Commission nullify the election and restrain Supreme Bishop de la Cruz from performing his functions. Six years later, in 1987, a Court of Appeals ruled in favor of Supreme Bishop de la Cruz as the validly-elected head of the PIC. Together with loyal bishops and priests, Former Supreme Bishop Ga created the *Iglesia Católica Filipina Independiente* (Philippine Independent Catholic Church)—another legal name of the PIC—exacerbating division and confusion within the church. Nearly 13 years later, he and his followers reconciled with the PIC on February 4, 1994.

Former Supreme Bishop Ga died on April 7, 2002 in Bacolod City.

Supreme Bishop Abdias de la Cruz

1981-1987

In a surprise upset, the PIC General Assembly of May 8, 1981 elected Supreme Bishop Abdias de la Cruz y Rebantad. During the entire six years of his service, his claim to leadership was challenged by his predecessor, who unsuccessfully petitioned for his removal.

Born on September 25, 1931, in Ochando, New Washington, Aklan, Abdias studied at St. Andrew's Theological Seminary, graduating with his bachelor of theology in 1956. He earned a second undergraduate degree in English from Far Eastern University in 1964 and a graduate degree in history from the University of the Philippines in 1967. At age 24, he was ordained to the diaconate on April 12, 1956. He was ordained to the priesthood less than four weeks later, on May 6, 1956. Father Abdias was consecrated to the episcopate on June 29, 1964 in La Paz, Iloilo.

His leadership as Supreme Bishop of the church began with the vexing challenge of maintaining unity in the church after the former Supreme Bishop's formation of a new Independent Catholic church. Recognizing how the National Priests Organization had consolidated power and opened the door for his election, Supreme Bishop de la Cruz established a close working relationship with the organization's clergy. He consulted with them to provide continuing education to clergy, particularly on the theme of recapturing the church's revolutionary nationalism.

The National Priests Organization provided support and counsel to Supreme Bishop de la Cruz, closely monitoring his decisions and actions. They violently objected when the Supreme Council of Bishops proposed the consecration of twelve priests to the episcopacy. The 2002 PIC History Committee notes, "the indifference between the organization and the church leadership…would not be over for more than a decade."[239]

While the legal challenge to his leadership continued, Supreme Bishop de la Cruz defended his central office from a violent takeover by Former Supreme Bishop Ga's clergy. At his request, Bishop Alberto Ramento led a group of seminarians, priests and lay people to eject the Former Supreme Bishop, who retaliated through the violent takeover of PIC parishes in Pandacan, Manila and Bacoor, Cavite.

Under Supreme Bishop de la Cruz' leadership in 1982, the PIC formed the Missionary Diocese of the United States and Canada, the first diocese of the PIC outside the Philippines.

After his leadership of the church, Former Supreme Bishop de la Cruz continued to serve as bishop of the diocese of Aklan and Capiz.

Supreme Bishop Solimán Ganno

1987-1989

In 1987, the PIC elected Supreme Bishop Solimán Ganno y Flores, who served until his death just over two years later.

Born on September 19, 1931 in Bungui, Ilocos Norte, Solimán completed his undergraduate studies at the University of Hawaii in 1953 and was ordained that year to the diaconate in Ilocos Norte. In 1954, he was ordained to the priesthood at the Church of Heroes and Martyrs in Sampaloc, Manila. He later earned his Bachelor of Theology from St. Andrew's Theological Seminary in 1965. In 1974, he earned his master of theology from the South East Asia Graduate School of Theology.

Father Solimán was consecrated to the episcopate on May 8, 1969, during the ceremony of inauguration of the new national cathedral in Manila. He was also named the first dean of the cathedral.

Bishop Ganno was later elected Supreme Bishop on May 8, 1987 in Bacoor, Cavite. The PIC History Committee states that his election was "a progressive and perceptive impulse for the Church to become a socially- and politically-relevant institution."[240]

On July 30, 1987, within three months of being elected, Supreme Bishop Ganno issued his Statement on Development, which set forth an agenda for renewal of the institutional life of the church. It also challenged Aglipayans to recapture their historical heritage and advocate for the marginalized.

During Supreme Bishop Ganno's leadership of the PIC, the Supreme Council of Bishops published two consecutive pastoral letters: "Our Heritage, Our Response" (1988), which articulated the nationalist heritage of the church, and "Witnessing: Sharing in the Pilgrimage" (1989). These pastoral letters reiterated the PIC's advocacy for its people and their agenda, support for nationalist industrialization and genuine land reform, and the condemnation of foreign intervention in the political governance of the country.

On May 19, 1989, after two years, Supreme Bishop Ganno died in Manila. Many accounts suggest that he died of heart failure at the altar of the national cathedral that morning. His unexpected death prevented him from seeing the fulfillment of the vision he set forth in his 1987 Statement on Development.

Supreme Bishop Tito Pasco

1989-1993

In light of the death of Former Supreme Bishop Solimán Ganno, the PIC General Assembly convened on June 22, 1989 to elect General Secretary Tito Pasco y Esquillo to the unexpired term of the former Supreme Bishop. Supreme Bishop Pasco served in this capacity for four years.

Born on January 4, 1930 in Balasan, Iloilo, Tito studied for much of 35 years. After earning his undergraduate degree in pre-law from Central Philippine University, he graduated with his bachelor of theology degree from St. Andrew's Theological Seminary in 1957. He was ordained to the diaconate on March 21, 1957 and to the priesthood on May 24, 1957. Father Tito earned a third undergraduate degree, in political science, from the University of Iloilo in 1964, and a graduate degree in history from the University of the Philippines in 1967.

While completing his third undergraduate degree, Father Tito was consecrated a bishop on March 31, 1964 at Our Lady of Peace Parish in La Paz, Iloilo. That same year, as a recently-consecrated bishop, Pasco attended the Wider Episcopal Fellowship Conference in Canterbury, England.[241]

Within two months of his election as Supreme Bishop in 1989, he made international news by launching a nationwide campaign to close all U.S. military bases in the Philippines and remove all nuclear weapons from the archipelago. One newspaper wrote that the Supreme Bishop, who led "a home-grown Philippine church claiming five million members," asked that his pastoral letter be read in all PIC churches throughout the nation.[242] A 1947 treaty between the United States and the Philippines was set to expire in 1992, and President Corazón Aquino contemplated renewal of the lease for the United States' oldest overseas facility, Subic Bay Naval Complex, and the largest American military installation overseas, Clark Air Base. Supreme Bishop Pasco argued that these bases violated Philippine sovereignty and were contrary to a constitutional provision that banned the storage of nuclear weapons in Philippine territory. A subsequent op-ed blasted Supreme Bishop Pasco's inability to see the benefits of the U.S. military presence in the archipelago—and shared disbelief that the PIC could number five million, or 8% of the Philippine population, without being listed in the *World Almanac*.[243]

In May 1990, the Supreme Council of Bishops published a document entitled, "Peace Building Mission of the *Iglesia Filipina Independiente*." The document addressed violence in the nation caused by the inequitable sharing of economic wealth, the fragmentation of the social system, military-political factionalism, and the proliferation of fundamentalist religious groups supporting the status quo. PIC bishops declared their churches as sanctuaries of the people, particularly for victims of war, and as "peace zones" where warring parties could engage in peace talks.

Meanwhile, Supreme Bishop Pasco continued the agenda of his predecessor and published his own Three-Year Vision Program, aimed to enhance stewardship and achieve self-reliance, self-governance and self-propagation for the church within three years. He launched this effort at the national cathedral on October 6, 1990. Two years later, he launched the Comprehensive National Program (CNP) to strengthen the church's organizational structures and processes.

In 1991, the PIC became involved in other social issues. Supreme Bishop Paso supported the teachers who camped at his national cathedral during a hunger strike, demanding better salaries and benefits from the Aquino administration—an event that inspired the 2001 movie, "Mila," featuring Maricel Soriano. When the issue of Filipina mail-order brides was exposed, the PIC, with strong leadership from its "Women of the National Cathedral," decried the prearranged marriages of Filipinas with foreigners. Later that year, the Supreme Council of Bishops asked the Aquino government to resume peace negotiations with the National Democratic Front.

To initiate a ten-year celebration leading up to the church's centennial celebration in 2002, Supreme Bishop Pasco launched the Centennial Decade Celebrations on August 3, 1992 and announced the "Decade Agenda" of the PIC. The 1993 Centennial Decade Celebration was hosted in Ilocos Norte.

After completing his term as Supreme Bishop, Pasco served as Bishop of the Diocese of Romblon and Mindoro until his retirement.

Supreme Bishop Alberto Ramento

1993-1999

Alberto Ramento y Baldovino was elected Supreme Bishop of the PIC in May 1993 and served in this capacity for six years.

Born on August 9, 1936 in Guimba, Nueva Ecija, Alberto earned his bachelor of theology from St. Andrew's Theological Seminary in 1958. He was ordained to the diaconate on April 8, 1958 and to the priesthood on April 28, 1958. In May 1969, Father Alberto was consecrated a bishop at the national cathedral in Manila. Over 20 years later, Bishop Ramento earned his master of divinity from St. Andrew's Theological Seminary in 1990.

Bishop Ramento was elected Supreme Bishop during the PIC's May 1993 General Assembly. As Supreme Bishop, he empowered laity, enhanced the church's stewardship efforts, and created various commissions for the church. He also led the PIC when it established a concordat with the Church of Sweden in 1995.

Under Supreme Bishop Ramento's leadership, the national Centennial Decade Celebrations continued: in Cagayan de Oro (1994), Iloilo City (1995), Cavite City (1996), Rosales, Pangasinan, (1997), Oroquieta (1998), and Cabadbaran, Agusan del Norte (1999). Significantly, the PIC approved the ordination of women in 1996 and ordained its first woman priest, Rev. Rosalina Rabaria, in 1997.

During Supreme Bishop Ramento's leadership, the PIC continued a theological articulation of its *Pro Deo et Patria* nationalist heritage. In May 1998, the Supreme Council of Bishops adopted two documents, "Towards a Common Vision of the *Iglesia Filipina Independiente*" and the "Statement on Aglipayan Spirituality." These documents speak clearly of the historical heritage of the church.

After Philippine President Joseph Estrada was elected in June 1998, the PIC issued a February 27, 1999 statement asking him to resume peace negotiations. On April 26, 1999, while peace talks broke down between the NDFP and GRP, the church issued another statement concerning its commitment to building peace. Hostilities resumed between the Philippine armed forces and the New People's Army, and Supreme Bishop Ramento, along with Bishops Romá Tiples, Felixberto Calang and Tomás Millamena helped facilitate the release of prisoners of war by the New People's Army in the Davao and Laguna provinces.

Former Supreme Bishop Ramento was instrumental in securing the release of various prisoners of war in Philippine revolutionary movements. He also served as a member of the Joint Monitoring Committee on the peace process between the National Democratic Front of the Philippines (NDFP) and the Government of the Republic of the Philippines (GRP).

Known as "the bishop of the poor, peasants and the oppressed," Supreme Bishop Ramento drew attention to the PIC's prophetic role in bringing a more just society to the Philippines. A critic of the Philippine government, he actively campaigned against human rights violations. He famously remarked, "I know [the government is] going to kill me next. But never will I abandon my duty to God and my ministry for the people."

Former Supreme Bishop Ramento was brutally stabbed to death while asleep in his home in Tarlac on October 3, 2007.[244] Left-wing groups decried his murder as a political killing, and his priests led chants while the people paraded his casket through the streets of Manila.[245] The PIC commemorates his martyrdom each October 3.

Supreme Bishop Tomás Millamena

1999-2005

Tomás Millamena y Amabrán was elected Supreme Bishop of the PIC in 1999 and served in this capacity through 2005.

Born on January 24, 1947 in Sibalom, Antique, Tomás studied at Central Philippine University. He was ordained to the diaconate on April 16, 1970, at the seminary chapel in Quezon City, and to the priesthood three days later, on April 19, 1970, at the national cathedral in Manila. He later earned a bachelor of theology from St. Andrew's Theological Seminary in 1978 and his master of divinity from the school in 1988.

After serving as associate pastor in Odiongan, Romblon for one year, Father Tomás was named pastor in Culasi, Antique in 1971. On March 6, 1982, Father Tomás was consecrated to the episcopacy at the Parish of St. Michael Archangel in Culasi and appointed bishop of the Diocese of Antique and Palawan. In 1995, he was appointed executive assistant to Supreme Bishop Alberto Ramento, then as General Secretary of the PIC. On May 8, 1999, Bishop Millamena was elected Supreme Bishop of the PIC.

Almost immediately, the new Supreme Bishop was involved in national politics, speaking out in July 1999 against the recruitment of his clergy as reservists for the Philippine Army. In September 1999, the PIC Executive Commission condemned the Estrada government for the unprincipled conduct of its military, which harassed and surveilled many PIC bishops and priests, alleging that they were listed in battle plans by the National People's Army. The military arrested Father Noel Dacuycuy and his wife, Mother Emelyn Gasco-Dacuycuy, as well as a PIC lay worker, Lorna Rivera-Baba,[246] alleging that they masterminded the December 1999 murder of Father Conrado Balweg, the Roman Catholic priest who co-founded the Cordillera People's Liberation Army.

In 2000 and 2001, Supreme Bishop Millamena joined with Philippine Senator Loren Legarda and Bishop Jesús Varela of the Roman Catholic Church to appeal to the National Democratic Front of the Philippines (NDFP) for the release of captives from the National People's Army (NPA). Filipinos elected President María Gloria Arroyo on January 20, 2001, and her administration immediately released NPA captives and resumed peace talks.

In 2000, the Philippine Statistics Authority enumerated 1,508,662 members of the Aglipayan church. Aglipayans possessed the fifth largest Christian denomination.[247]

On April 8, 2001, Supreme Bishop Millamena led a group of PIC clergy and members of the National Council of Churches in the Philippines in welcoming the NDFP negotiating panel at the Philippines. Ten days later, a number of PIC clergy and laity attended the Conference for Genuine and Lasting Peace, hosted by the National Council of Churches in the Philippines (NCCP) and the Roman Catholic Bishops Conference in the Philippines (CBCP). As Supreme Bishop, he played a significant role in peace negotiations between the National Democratic Front of the Philippines (NDFP) and the Government of the Republic of the Philippines (GRP) in Oslo, Norway on April 27-30, 2001. Unafraid to take principled stands, he attended other peace talks in Oslo as well, excoriating the GRP for walking away from negotiations after the punishment of the notorious torturer Colonel Rodolfo Aguinaldo in June 2001.

Under Supreme Bishop Millamena's leadership, the Centennial Decade Celebrations continued in Dumaguete (2000). In 2001, to mark the 99th anniversary of the PIC, local dioceses marked the annual Centennial Decade Celebrations. Because he served as Supreme Bishop during the church's centennial celebration on August 2-3, 2002, he is referred to as the "Centenary Supreme Bishop."

In 2002, Supreme Bishop Millamena shared a ten-year strategic plan for the church, which included episcopal study-conferences, regional clergy convocations, and lay congresses.

On January 8, 2003, more than 100 years after the church's creation, the PIC ended disputes over the PIC name, finally claiming exclusive right to its name by filing with the Philippine Securities and Exchange Commission,

After completing his two terms of office, Supreme Bishop Millamena oversaw the Dioceses of Laguna and Iloilo, and took place in peace negotiations when they resumed in Oslo in 2004.

On June 4, 2014, Former Supreme Bishop Millamena died of cirrhosis of the liver. One consultant of the NDFP/GRP peace process likened his struggle to the struggle of his nation, noting that he

> fought a continuous battle against cancer. Cancer killed his
> body, but his valuable lifelong contributions in the battle

against social cancer—and for national liberation, justice, equality, social upliftment and lasting peace in the life of his beloved people—continue even after his physical passing away.[248]

Upon news of his death, the NDFP praised Former Supreme Bishop Millamena's

staunch advocacy for a just and lasting peace in the Philippines and his firm pro-people stand against the anti-people and anti-national policies of the U.S.-Aquino regime and other earlier reactionary regimes....In speeches at various national and international forums, he did not hesitate to expose the role of U.S. imperialism in the exploitation and oppression of the Filipino people....We are certain that his closeness to the struggling Filipino people and his dedication to a just and lasting peace in the Philippines will be a lasting legacy and inspiration to those who continue the struggle for national and social liberation and a just and lasting peace[249]

After his passing, the PIC stated:

His consistent voice on many social and political issues has raised the consciousness and placed these important issues at the heart of every clergy and member of the *Iglesia Filipina Independiente*....In the challenge of many crosses, crowns of thorns and iron nails, he always lifted the presence of the living Christ among the people.[250]

The Christians for National Liberation praised Former Supreme Bishop Millamena as inspiring "the legions…who are engaged in the continuing struggle for national democratic revolution with a socialist perspective in this our beloved land."[251] The "hero of the toiling masses,"[252] Former Supreme Bishop Millamena is remembered as humble and humorous, soft-spoken but uncompromising, and radiating the comforting presence of God.[253]

Supreme Bishop Godofredo David

2007-2011

Godofredo David y Juico was elected Supreme Bishop of the PIC on May 10, 2005 and served in this capacity through 2011.

As Supreme Bishop, he continued the implementation of his predecessor's ten-year strategic plan, focusing on human resource development, worker benefits, property consolidations, and the strengthening of regional structures and ecumenical partnerships.

In 2006, Supreme Bishop David met with Episcopal Presiding Bishop Frank Griswold in Columbus, Ohio, to update the 1997 concordat between their churches.

The PIC website further states that "the extrajudicial killing of the Most Reverend Alberto Ramento in 2006 has led [Supreme Bishop David's] administration toward a more pro-active engagement with justice and peace, and human rights issues."[254]

In 2010, the Philippines census enumerated 916,639 members of the Aglipayan church. Aglipayans comprised roughly one percent of the Philippine population and possessed the sixth largest Christian denomination.[255]

After serving as Supreme Bishop, David oversaw the Diocese of Rizal and Pampanga.

Supreme Bishop Ephraim Fajutagana

2011-2017

Ephraim Fajutagana y Servañez was elected Supreme Bishop of the PIC on May 10, 2011 and served in this capacity through 2017.

Born in Odiongan, Romblon, Ephraim earned his bachelor of theology from St. Andrew's Theological Seminary in 1977 and was ordained to the priesthood the same year.

Father Ephraim was consecrated to the episcopacy in July 2002 and served the Diocese of Romblon and Mindoros. After acting as General Secretary of the PIC, Bishop Fajutagana was elected Supreme Bishop on May 10, 2011 and installed at the national cathedral on June 11.

Three days later, Supreme Bishop Fajutagana joined a march to the Department of Justice to demand justice for PIC lay leader and activist Benjamin Bayles, who was a victim of an extra-judicial killing on June 14, 2010. The demonstration was co-hosted by the PIC, the National Council of Churches in the Philippines (NCC), the United Church of Christ in the Philippines (UCCP), and the Promotion of Church People's Response (PCPR). On that occasion the PIC Executive Commission announced its creation of the Bayles National Task Force to address extrajudicial killings, disappearances, and "the ever-worsening human rights violations in the Philippines."

On August 2-3, 2011, the PIC's South Central Luzon Conference hosted the church's 109th Proclamation Anniversary, with an estimated 5,000 clergy and faithful from seven dioceses in attendance.

On September 1, 2011, Supreme Bishop Fajutagana commemorated the 71st death anniversary of First Supreme Bishop Gregorio Aglípay. During his homily at the Aglipayan shrine in the Diocese of Batac, he spoke of "the spirit of Gregorio Aglípay — the spirit that seeks justice as the foundation of peace in a society that is battered by aggression and violence — that every member of the *Iglesia Filipina Independiente* must strive to live out."

On September 12-15, 2011, Supreme Bishop Fajutagana participated in the meeting of the Supreme Council of Bishops at the Parish of Saint Anthony of Padua in Presentación, Camarines Sur. The event began with a procession by clergy and laity, followed by a solemn eucharist led by Supreme Bishop Fajutagana.

On October 3, 2011, Supreme Bishop Fajutagana commemorated the fifth anniversary of the death of Former Supreme Bishop Alberto Ramento. The event at the national cathedral included a renewed call for justice. The previous day, the Old Catholic Church of the Netherlands marked the occasion with its own solemn mass and commemoration of Supreme Bishop Ramento "and all other martyrs in the movement of justice, peace and integrity of creation in the Philippines." The event in the Netherlands was co-sponsored by Filipino Parish Netherlands (FPNL), a faith community of expatriates first gathered by Haarlem Bishop Dick Schoon on June 19, 2011, on the occasion of the 150th anniversary of the birth of José Rizal.[256] Two weeks later, on October 18, representatives of the PIC met with Department of Justice Secretary Leila de Lima, who expressed support for securing justice in the extrajudicial killing. Father César Taguba, Chair of the Filipino Parish Council Netherlands (FPCNL) in Amsterdam, similarly urged the Aquino government to stop the extrajudicial killings that resulted in the deaths of over 30 Filipino church leaders and workers from January 2001 to October 2011.

On February 12, 2012, Supreme Bishop Fajutagana attended a service with Presiding Bishop Katharine Jefferts Schori of the Episcopal Church in Bangao, in the northern Philippines. The occasion also commemorated the 15th anniversary of the concordat of full communion between the two churches on February 17, 1997. Representatives of the two churches met again on April 16-17, 2012 in Safety Harbor, Florida, to revisit the updated concordat of full communion signed by Supreme Bishop Godofredo David in 2006.

In May 2012, Supreme Bishop Fajutagana traveled to London, where he met with Archbishop of Canterbury Dr. Rowan Williams in the office of the Archbishop of York.

In October 2012, the PIC commemorated the sixth anniversary of the martyrdom of Former Supreme Bishop Ramento with a two-day conference on church mission and human rights. Co-sponsored by the Ramento Project for Rights Defenders (RPRD) of the South Central Luzon Bishops Conference, the event attracted 80 PIC bishops, priests and lay leaders, as well as representatives of the Old Catholic Church of the Netherlands, the Old Catholic Church of

Germany, the Church of Sweden, and the Anglican Church of Melanesia.

In 2012, the PIC actively advocated for the Responsible Parenthood and Reproductive Health Act of 2012, which guarantees universal access to contraception and sex education. Vigorously opposed by the Roman Catholic Church in the Philippines, the legislation was enacted on December 23, 2012.

On June 14, 2013, the PIC hosted a liturgical forum at the national cathedral to commemorate the death of slain lay activist Benjamin Bayles. The next month, on July 23, 2013, the church hosted a forum on the political persecution of churches. Seventy bishops, priests and lay leaders attended the discussion on the recent harassment of Bishop Antonio Ablon of the Pagadian Diocese and Father Terry Revollido, Rector of Aglípay Central Theological Seminary (ACTS) in the Dagupan Diocese.

On August 8, 2014, Archbishop of Canterbury Justin Welby visited the PIC cathedral in Manila and reaffirmed the concordat of full communion between the Church of England and the Aglipayan church.

In 2015, the Philippine Statistics Authority enumerated 756,225 members of the Aglipayan church. Aglipayans possessed the sixth largest Christian denomination. More men (384,767) than women (371,458) were recorded as members of the church.

Supreme Bishop Fajutagana made international news in January 2016 after a visit from Philippine senator and vice presidential candidate Ferdinand Marcos, Jr., son of the late dictator, who announced the PIC's endorsement of his candidacy. Supreme Bishop Fajutagana, who shared a pastoral letter earlier that month warning bishops and priests to beware of politicians soliciting their endorsement, expressed dismay that his gesture of welcoming the senator was misconstrued as an endorsement by the church.[257] The same article suggested that the PIC was comprised of "at least two million members" at the time.

In February 2017, the PIC shared a document, "Our Common Humanity, Our Shared Dignity," recognizing LGBTIQ+ persons — the preferred, inclusive term of the church. This document stressed the church's position that it "must openly embrace God's people of all sexes, sexual orientations, gender identities and expressions." The statement acknowledged the PIC's "history of indifference toward the LGBTIQ+ people [who] feel less human, [and more] discriminated against and stigmatized. We apologize for instances they felt that, through our thoughts, words and deeds, God's love is selective."[258] According to *Outrage Magazine*, the push for this document originated during the 2014 PIC General Assembly, when a gay man inquired into the church's plan for addressing sexual minorities.[259] The president and executive vice president of the PIC's youth organization continued their advocacy on the issue. Vaughn Geuseppe Alviar, moderator of IFI Bahaghari Conversations, shared four drafts of the document, considered a brave statement in a nation long influenced by conservative Roman Catholic forces. *Outrage* noted the support of the PIC for Pride marches, HIV/AIDS screenings and activities, and condom distribution.

Supreme Bishop Rhee Millena Timbang

2017-

After serving as Bishop of the Diocese of Surigao, Rhee Millena Timbang was elected Supreme Bishop of the PIC in May 2017. Before he was elected, he served as Chair of the Supreme Council of Bishops.

An advocate for gender equality, Supreme Bishop Millena led the PIC through the process of consecrating the first woman bishop in its 117-year history. Having approved the ordination of women in 1996, the PIC counted on the ministry of some 30 women presbyters and 10 women deacons by 2019. On May 5, 2019, Supreme Bishop Millena consecrated Bishop Emelyn Dacuycuy at the Cathedral and National Shrine of St. Mary in Batac, Ilocos Norte. Various co-consecrators from the Episcopal Church in the United States and the Church of Sweden participated in her historic consecration.

Appropriately, Bishop Dacuycuy leads the diocese — initially of all male clergy — where the PIC's revolutionary first supreme bishop, Gregorio Aglípay, was born. Speaking of her long journey to the episcopate, which involved eleven special meetings of the General Assembly and three meetings of the Supreme Council of Bishops, Bishop Dacuycuy, who prefers to emphasize her womanhood by being called Bishop Emelyn,[260] shared,

> Patriarchy and *machismo* are still prevalent in the Philippine culture. Filipino women are not yet fully free from economic, political, cultural and religious oppression. The work of empowering women must be continued vigorously.[261]

Bishop Emelyn imagined her place on the Supreme Council of Bishops as "a female dragon entering a den of lions, but it turned out to be a very pleasant, amiable and largely enthusiastic reception."[262] After the consecration, Supreme Bishop Millena noted,

> In the past, many bishops were reluctant to elect a woman priest to the episcopate because they feared the possibility that [women] can become Supreme Bishop. Ironically, it is this possibility which made Emelyn's election a reality and the change that the church hopes to see…. I do not mind a woman bishop becoming Supreme Bishop someday.[263]

Bishop Emelyn summarizes,

> My greatest joy is to serve in a church that welcomes all and gives everyone an opportunity to serve. Gender is just a social construct, a way of ordering society and ascribing values. As a spiritual community, however, we must see beyond gender. We must see God's people as Jesus sees them—children of God and heirs of God's eternal reign.[264]

The Aglipayan Church Today

After the Roman Catholic Church, the Philippine Independent Church is one of the largest Christian denomination in the Philippines today. Estimates of the number of Aglipayans widely vary. The PIC suggests that more than six million Filipinos may self-identify as Aglipayan—five percent of Filipinos—both in the Philippines and in Filipino diasporas in the United States, Canada, Europe, Asia and the Middle East.[265] In contrast, the 2010 Philippine national census reported 916,639 Aglipayans, roughly one percent of the population, though an estimated 3.9 million Filipinos were not reported by the census.[266] The 2010 census ranked the Aglipayan church after 74 million Roman Catholics, nearly 2.5 million evangelicals, and over one million Protestants of the National Council of Churches in the Philippines.

According to the World Council of Churches, the PIC operates two colleges (in Manila and in Southern Leyte), three theological seminaries, 14 primary and secondary schools, and several kindergartens. The World Council of Churches says of the PIC:

> It is much involved in peace-building ministry, human and democratic rights advocacy and ecumenical linkages. It pursues better Christian education and stewardship; the training of more dedicated priests and more aggressive campaigns against all forms of poverty are high on its agenda. Among its program objectives, the IFI seeks to fully inform its members of its history, mission and ministry, to enhance the interaction between national, diocesan and local levels, to establish effective instruments for the implementation of its activities and to achieve recognition as a pillar of Philippine society.[267]

The PIC is governed by its General Assembly, which meets every three years and authorizes the Executive Commission, chaired by the Supreme Bishop, to act on its behalf in the interim. Other members of the Executive Commission include the General Secretary, the chairs of the National Lay Council, Commission on Programs and Projects, and Commission on Business and Finance, five bishops elected by the Supreme Council of Bishops, five priests elected by the Council of Priests, and the three presidents of the PIC's national organizations of men, women and youth.

Elected by the General Assembly, the Supreme Bishop serves as primate of the church, presiding over the National Cathedral of the Holy Child in Manila. The Supreme Bishop is currently elected for a six-year term and cannot be re-elected. In consultation with the Executive Commission, the Supreme Bishop speaks on issues of faith and morals.

The Supreme Council of Bishops includes all active and retired bishops, who work together to define doctrinal orthodoxy, prescribe liturgy, and provide pastoral and moral guidance. PIC bishops are organized into four regional conferences. They preside over the PIC's 47 dioceses, which includes the Diocese of the Eastern and Western United States and Canada.

Comprised entirely of priests, the Council of Priests promotes the welfare of clergy and represents their interests and concerns to the General Assembly.

Appendix A

Aglipayan Declaration of Faith & Articles of Religion

We, the Bishops, Priests and lay members, delegates to the General Assembly of the Philippine Independent Church, held in the City of Manila on the 5th day of August, A.D. 1947, do reiterate our Faith and publicly declare that WE BELIEVE IN

The Holy Trinity

One God, true and living, of infinite power, wisdom and goodness; the Maker and Preserver of all things visible and invisible. And that in the unity of this Godhead there be three Persons, of one substance, power and eternity: the Father who is made of none, neither created nor begotten; the Son who is of the Father alone, not made nor created, but begotten; the Holy Ghost who is of the Father and the Son, neither made, nor created, nor begotten, but proceeding.

Jesus Christ, the only-begotten Son of God

Jesus Christ, the only-begotten Son of God, the second Person of the Trinity, very and eternal God, of one substance with the Father, took [our] nature in the womb of the Blessed Virgin, after she had conceived by the Holy Ghost. He suffered under Pontius Pilate, was crucified, died and was buried. He descended into hell. The third day he rose again from the dead, He ascended into Heaven, and sitteth at the right hand of God the Father Almighty; from thence He shall come to judge both the living and the dead.

The Holy Spirit

The Holy Spirit, the Lord and Giver of life, Who proceedeth from the Father and the Son: Who with the Father and the Son together we worship and glorify.

One, Catholic and Apostolic Church

The Church, Holy, Catholic and Apostolic, which is the Body of Christ, founded by Christ for the redemption and sanctification of [humankind], and to which Church He gave power and authority to preach His Gospel to the whole world under the guidance of His Holy Spirit.

We hold to the following **Articles of Religion** taught by this Church:

1. **Salvation**. Salvation is obtained only through a vital faith in Jesus Christ, the Son of God, as Lord and Savior. This faith should manifest itself in good works.

2. **Holy Scriptures**. The Holy Scriptures contain all things necessary to salvation, and nothing which cannot be proved thereby should be required to be believed.

3. **The Creeds**. The Articles of the Christian Faith as contained in the ancient Creeds known as the Apostles' and Nicene Creeds are to be taught by this Church and accepted by the faithful.

4. **The Sacraments**. The Sacraments are outward and visible signs of our faith and a means whereby God manifests His goodwill towards us and confers grace upon us. Two Sacraments, Baptism and Holy Communion, commonly called the Mass, ordained by Christ Himself, are held to be generally necessary to salvation.

   - **Baptism** is necessary for salvation. It signifies and confers grace, cleansing from original sin as well as actual sin previously committed; makes us children of God and heirs of everlasting life. It effects our entrance into the Church of God. It is administered with water in the Name of the Father, the Son, and the Holy Ghost.

   - **Confirmation**, whereby, through the imposition of the Bishop's hands, anointing and prayer, baptized Christians are strengthened by the gifts of the Holy Spirit and confirmed in the Faith.

   - **Penance**, the confession of sins as commanded by Jesus Christ.

   - The **Holy Eucharist**, the sacrament of the Body and Blood of Christ, taken and received by the faithful for the strengthening and refreshing of their bodies and souls.

   - **Holy Unction**, whereby the sick, especially one in danger of death, is anointed with oil during prayer. He receives, if necessary, remission of sins, the strengthening of his soul, and, if it be God's will, restoration to health.

- **Holy Orders**, a sacrament by which bishops, priests and deacons are ordained and receive power and authority to perform their sacred duties.

- **Holy Matrimony**, a sacrament in which [two] are joined together in the holy estate of matrimony.

5. **The Holy Eucharist**. The Holy Eucharist, commonly called the Mass, is the central act of Christian worship. It is the sacrament of our redemption by Christ's death. Those who partake of it receive the Body and Blood of Christ. All who purpose to make their communion should diligently try and examine themselves before they presume to eat of that Bread and drink of that Cup. For as the benefit is great, if with a true penitent heart and lively faith a man receive that Holy Sacrament, so is the danger great if he receive the same unworthily. The Mass is to be said in the official language of the Church in such a way it can be heard by the worshipers. The authorized Order for the celebration of the Mass is that set forth in the Prayer Book adopted by this Church.

6. **Sacred Ministry**. From Apostolic times there have been three orders of ministers in the Church of God: bishops, priests and deacons. These orders are to be reverently esteemed and continued in this Church. And no man is to be accepted as a lawful Bishop, Priest, or Deacon in this Church, or permitted to execute any functions pertaining to these Orders, except he be called, tried, examined, and admitted thereunto according to the canons of this Church, and in accordance with the Order prescribed by this Church for making, Ordaining and consecrating bishops, priests and deacons, or has had Episcopal consecration or ordination.

7. **Celibacy of the Clergy**. Bishops, priests, and deacons are not commanded by God's law to marry or to abstain from marriage, therefore they are permitted to marry at their own discretion, as they shall judge the same to serve better to godliness.

8. **Church Building**. Churches for the worship of God are to be erected and separated from all unhallowed, worldly, and

common uses, that people may reverence the Majesty of God and show forth greater devotion and humility in His service.

9. **The Altar**. The altar is the most sacred part of the Church because there Jesus is sacramentally present. It symbolizes Mt. Calvary, and, therefore, if images of Saints are used for adornment, care is to be exercised that such ornaments may not distract the minds of the worshipers from the Person of Jesus Christ.

10. **Worship, Rites and Ceremonies**. Only such orders of service as have been authorized by this Church shall be used in Public Worship; provided, however, that the Diocesan Bishop or Supreme Council of Bishops may authorize Orders of Service for special occasions.

11. **Language of Public Service**. All public services shall be conducted in the official language of the Church, or in any other language the Supreme Council of Bishops may prescribe.

12. **Purity of Life**. Holiness, altruism, obedience to God's Commandments and a zeal for His honor and glory are incumbent upon Clergy and Laity alike, therefore all should be trained in a clean and disciplined life, not neglecting prayer, study, and the exercise of moral discipline.

13. **Knowledge**. All truth is of God, therefore the Church should promote sound knowledge and good learning. No books except those detrimental to good morals are to be prohibited.

14. **The Blessed Virgin**. The Virgin Mary was chosen by God to be the Mother of Jesus Christ. As Jesus Christ is truly God and Mary is the Mother of Jesus Christ, she is the Mother of God in His human generation. She whom God honored is to be honored above all.

15. **The Saints**. Persons universally recognized for their holiness of life, loyalty and courage, especially the Blessed Virgin and the New Testament Saints, are to be held in reverent remembrance. Veneration of Saints is not contrary to God's commandments as revealed in the Scriptures; but their deification is condemned by the Church as a monstrous blasphemy. Veneration of the Saints must not obscure the duty

of the faithful to direct approach to God through Jesus Christ. Honor rendered the Saints must in no wise detract from the honor due the Three Persons of the Holy Trinity.

16. **Miracles**. Holy Scriptures teach us that events take place in the natural world, but out of its established order, which are possible only through the intervention of divine power, like the Incarnation of Jesus Christ. So-called miracles, based not on well-authenticated facts but on merely fantastic rumors, are repudiated. Belief in unsubstantiated miracles leads to pagan fanaticism and is to be condemned as destructive to the true faith.

17. **Attitude Towards The Roman Church**. When this Church withdrew from the Roman Catholic Church, it repudiated the authority of the pope and such doctrines, customs and practices as were inconsistent with the Word of God, sound learning and a good conscience. It had no intention of departing from Catholic doctrine, practice and discipline as set forth by the Councils of the undivided Church. Such departures as occurred were due to the exigencies of the times, and are to be corrected by official action as opportunity affords, so that this Church may be brought into the stream of historic Christianity and be universally acknowledge as a true branch of the Catholic Church.

18. **Attitude Towards Other Churches**. Opportunity is to be sought for closer cooperation with other branches of the Catholic Church, and cordial relations maintained with all who acknowledge Jesus Christ as Lord and Savior.

19. **Church and State**. This Church is politically independent of the State, and the State of the Church. The Church does not ally itself with any particular school of political thought or with any political party. Its members are politically free and are urged to be exemplary citizens and to use their influence for the prosperity and welfare of the State.

20. **Doctrine and Constitutional Rules of the Church and the Fundamental Epistles**. The Doctrine and Constitutional Rules of the Philippine Independent Church, adopted on October 28th, 1903, and subsequently amended, and the Fundamental Epistles of the Philippine Independent Church, are henceforth

not to be held as binding either upon the Clergy or Laity of this Church in matters of Doctrine, Discipline or Order, wherein they differ in substance from the Declaration of Faith or the Articles of Religion contained herein. They are to be valued as historical documents promulgated by the Founders of this Church when they were seeking to interpret the Catholic Faith in a manner understood by the people. Under the inspiration of the Holy Spirit the Church has sought to eradicate such errors of judgment and doctrine as crept into its life and official documents in times past.

21. **Additions, Amendments, Repeal**. The Declaration of Faith shall not be altered, amended or repealed. However, the Articles of Religion may be amended, repealed or added to by an absolute majority of the delegates to the General Assembly having the right to vote. Such action before it becomes binding upon the Church must be ratified by the Supreme Council of Bishops and approved by the Supreme Bishop.

Appendix B

Aglipayan Mission, Vision, Goals & Strategies

The 2014 ten-year strategic plan of the Aglipayan Church notes the following:

<u>Our Mission</u>
The *Iglesia Filipina Independiente*, as a community of faith steeped in the nationalist history of the workers and Filipino people's struggle in the Philippines, affirms its historical mission and ministry to empower the poor, deprived and oppressed through liberative education, organizing, and mobilizing the Filipino people to pursue life in its fullness, and to be active witnesses against injustices and for the propagation of God's love to all humankind.

<u>Our Vision</u>
Consistent with the IFI's belief in the purity of life, holiness, altruism and obedience to God's commandments and the church's history and mandate of being one in the people's struggle for liberation, the IFI envisions a global community of men and women working together toward the fullness of life and respect for the dignity of all peoples and nations, the promotion of the integrity of all creation, and the pursuit of justice and peace.

<u>Our Goals</u>
1. Education, worship and ministry for strengthening the membership's (clergy and laity) knowledge in IFI history and teachings, both spiritual and phenomenal.

   Strategies
   A. Deepening and enhancing the expression of Aglipayan Spirituality through participation in our collective fight against injustices/human rights violations.

B. Engaging in liturgical renewal towards a more intensive education and propagation of our faith.

C. Further asserting our own perspective through giving more emphasis in reading the context of the historical events that gave birth to the IFI, its ministry and mission.

D. Coming up with common and official resource materials that are relevant to the propagation of our faith.

E. Enhancing understanding of Church membership on Declaration of Faith and Articles of Religion and propagate it to all members.

F. Developing well-informed, active and responsive church members through Christian Education that reflects Aglipayan Spirituality.

G. Implementing and evolving a comprehensive human resource development program for both the clergy and lay.

2. Education, worship and ministry for strengthening the membership's (clergy and laity) knowledge in IFI history and teachings, both spiritual and phenomenal.

Strategy

A. Developing the National Program: program and institutional strengthening of current development programs being implemented (Rights Defenders, HIV/AIDS Awareness, Relief and Rehab, psychosocial intervention TFER/BK, Community Development Program (IDP and ABCD), Livelihood and Cottage Industry, WAP to name a few, in support to the struggle of the basic sectors.

3. Stewardship and resources development in supporting the work of the Church at all levels.

   Strategies

   A. Establishing tithing as the minimum standard form of Christian giving.

   B. Popularization of the church strategy for stewardship and resource development.

   C. Implementation of the church strategy for stewardship and resource development.

   D. Enhancing education on Centralization of Funds and Resource Management.

   E. Maximum use of idle properties.

   F. Reviewing and Systematizing policies on program implementation.

   G. Staff for TYSP implementation.

4. Concordat and international ecumenical work for strengthening solidarity relations with other Churches and faith-based institutions.

   Strategies

   A. Celebrating the Jubilee of Concordat Relations in 2015.

   B. Engaging in discussions on the World Council of Churches' document on Baptism Eucharist and Ministry with other Christian denominations specially with NCCP member-churches.

   C. Enhancing concordat relations with Concordat Churches.

   D. Pursue relationship with Evangelical Lutheran Church in America (ELCA).

   E. Exploring on strengthening South-South Relations with Churches in the South.

Appendix C

Aglipayan Spirituality

Aglipayan Spirituality is our holistic response to the call of the God of salvation to liberate His people from all forms of dehumanization. It is our relationship with God, with the community and with the rest of creation rooted in the Judeo-Christian faith and tradition. It is living out the mandate of the Gospel of Christ and our historical heritage of serving God and Country (*Pro Deo et Patria*).

Aglipayan Spirituality is rooted in the life and teachings of Jesus Christ, continuously inspired by the Holy Spirit, manifested in the life of Bishop Gregorio Aglípay and in the lives of the founding forebears of the IFI.

It is a life of prayer centered in Christ, faithful to the Gospel, inspired and sustained by the Holy Spirit.

Aglipayan Spirituality is our continuing pilgrimage with the liberating God towards the fulfillment of the mission and ministry of the *Iglesia Filipina Independiente*, for the transformation of church and society and for the renewal and rebirthing of the whole creation. It affirms our hope for the establishment of the Kingdom of God here on earth.

The *Iglesia Filipina Independiente*, as a pilgrim Church, compelled by her spirituality, actively participates in the realization of the Kingdom of God.

Aglipayan Spirituality, inspired by the message of God "to do justice, love kindness and walk humbly with Him" (Micah 6:8), is our commitment to serve God and His people in the struggle for freedom, justice, peace and total human development. A commitment whose basis is the critical and scientific analysis of the structures and systems that perpetuates the continuing destruction of life, a commitment being nurtured through immersion and solidarity with the basic masses.

It is our service to the liberating God concretized in solidarity with the Filipino people in their struggle for peace, justice, freedom and abundant life.

Appendix D

Aglipayan Mission

The following document is found on the PIC website as a statement on church mission.

I. What is the Church
1. By the Church we mean primarily, the *ecclesia* or assembly which God has called out to be His people, founded by Jesus Christ organized hierarchically in a visible ministry of Bishops, Priests and Deacons by means of an unbroken line of apostolic succession, and which exists as the mystical body of Christ (Eph. 1:22;5:23-30; Col. 1:18,24; 1 Cor. 12:12-31; Rom. 12:4), serving to advance the Kingdom of God and the salvation of [humankind].
2. In the fullest sense, the Church is the creation of God with Jesus Christ as its head and receiving its life from the Holy Spirit by whose operations its members are incorporated into one body by baptism, and its ministers are ordained through apostolic laying-on of hands.
3. The Church is One, Holy, Apostolic and Catholic assembled under the Father and united in the Holy Spirit, and which exists as the Body of Christ, mystically extended to [all].
4. She is the sacrament of the unity and union of [humankind] with God because of her relationship with God and Jesus Christ, its Head and Savior. The Church is also described as the "bride of Christ", she it was whom he "delivered and gave himself up for her that he might sanctify her... without spot or wrinkle or any such thing, that she might be holy and without blemish" (Eph. 5:23;26-27;32).
5. The Church on earth is a pilgrim who goes out with faith and looks forward to the city with which he has foundation, whose builder and maker is God (Heb. 11:10) who calls all to repentance and salvation in God, because her organization and institution constitute the method and the sacramental means which God employs in exercising His sovereignty over those who accept His Kingdom.
6. The Church is a tract to be cultivated, the field of God (1 Cor. 3:9) on which the ancient olive tree grows. Its holy roots are

patriarchs and in her, the reconciliation of Jew and Gentile was brought about and will be brought about (Rom. 11:13-26). The Church has been cultivated by the heavenly vinedresser as His chosen vineyard (Mat. 21:33-43). The true vine is Christ who gave life and fruitfulness to the branches, that is us.

II. The Church as Mission

7. The Church, being called by God to be His people, is also sent. By virtue of His divine "calling" and "sending", she is missionary in character.

8. God, out of His steadfast love, sent His only begotten Son to the world, "not to condemn the world but so the world might be saved through Him". He sent his only begotten Son to seek and save the lost and that "whoever believes in Him should not perish but have eternal life" (Jn. 3:16; Lk. 19:10).

9. The Son, therefore, through whom we became adopted children of God (Rom. 8:16-17), and in whom all things shall be reestablished (Eph. 1:4-5, 10) came in accordance with the will of the Father. Through Him and in Him, God revealed Himself so that the world might be reconciled to Him. The *Iglesia Filipina Independiente* has the mission of revealing, unmasking and proclaiming the One and True God" in whom we live and move and have our being" (Acts 17-28) in the hearts, minds, culture and life of the Filipino people (Acts 17:22ff). By this shall Filipinos know that He is God who created and redeemed the world, who blessed us with this country and with this Filipino Church and thus draw us unto Him.

10. In order to fulfill the will of the Father, Christ proclaimed and inaugurated the Kingdom of God. He offered himself on the cross in obedience to the will of the Father (Lk. 22:42) that he might draw all to himself (Jn. 12:32). The Church continues this sacrifice of the cross every time and in every place during the Eucharist, in which the unity of the Church is expressed and brought about (1 Cor. 10:17).

11. When Christ has been lifted up from the earth, He sent the Holy Spirit from God on Pentecost in order that what He has inaugurated might be proclaimed and continued until the end of time (Mt. 28:18) and that he might sanctify her and lead her into all truth (Jn. 14:16;16:13).

12. By her very nature and the divine command of Christ (Mt. 28:19-20), the Church on earth is on a mission, just as Christ was sent on a mission according to the will of the Father. The Church is called and sent to follow the path of Christ to proclaim to all men and women the saving work of God "until all be fulfilled in his kingdom", and that "at the name of Jesus every knee should bow and every tongue confess that Jesus Christ is Lord, to the glory of God the Father" (Phil 2:10).

13. The missionary zeal and dynamism of the Church is bestowed upon her by the indwelling of the Holy Spirit. It is renewed and revitalized in the celebration of the Eucharist where "Christ our Passover is sacrificed for us " (1 Cor. 5:7b) and in which all members of the one Body are commissioned to "go out into the world to love and serve the Lord" strengthened by the fellowship of the Holy Spirit (1 Cor. 3:16; Acts 2:17-18, 4:31,9:31).

III. Biblical Basis of Mission

A. "I am the Lord, I have called you in righteousness, I have taken you by the hand and kept you; I have given you as a covenant to the people, a light to the nations" (Isa. 42:6).

B. "The Spirit of the Lord God is upon me, because the Lord has anointed me to bring good tidings to the afflicted; he has sent me to bind up the broken hearted, to proclaim liberty to the captives, and the opening of the prison to those who are bound; to proclaim the year of the Lord's favor" (Isa. 61:1-2a).

C. "As the Father has sent me even so I send you... Receive the Holy Spirit" (Jn. 20:21-22).

D. "Go therefore and make disciples of all nations, baptizing them in the name of the Father and of the Son and the Holy Spirit; teaching them to observe all that I have commanded you; and do, I am with you always, to the close of the age." (Mt. 28:19-20).

IV. IFI Concept of Mission

14. Mission is primarily of God. It is God's action in the world in Jesus Christ and in the Holy Spirit. It is God's activity in which the Church participates by the power of the Holy Spirit to baptize, (Eph. 1:10) so that God's Kingdom shall be proclaimed and established for all times and in all places. Just as the "word (Christ) became flesh and dwelt among us, full of grace and

truth" (Jn. 1:14) so the IFI's mission is primarily incarnational. The IFI should bear in mind that the Lord Jesus Christ" who though; he was in form of God, did not count equality with God a thing grasped, but emptied himself, taking the form of a servant, being born in likeness of men. And being found in human form he humbled himself and became obedient unto death, even death on the across" (Phil 2:5-8). So the Church has to incarnate herself into where the people are. She has to take seriously the context where she is situated and wherever the Spirit of God leads her.

15. It is from the mission of the Son and the Holy Spirit that the Church takes her origin according to the will of God the Father. It is God through the Holy Spirit who initiates mission. The indwelling of the Holy Spirit in the Church (1 Cor. 3:16) is her life and power for mission (Mt. 28:20; Acts 1:16). What the Church hopes, therefore, is not her work but the work of the Holy Spirit.

16. Mission is also the incessant flow of the edifying love of God revealed and expressed in the person and work of Jesus Christ. This divine human activity in which the Church participates is essentially the proclamation of and witness to the Gospel of Jesus Christ. This mandate concerns basically:

    A. [Humankind] – our life and the imperative need for conversion to Christ; and

    B. The building of the Kingdom of God.

17. Christ sent the Holy Spirit from the Father that the saving work of God in Him might be constituted beginning from Jerusalem to the ends of the earth (Acts 18). It is this same Holy Spirit that came down upon the apostles on Pentecost to remain with them forever. It is the same Spirit that impels the Church to mission, just as Christ is impelled to the work of His ministry when the Holy Spirit descended upon Him at His baptism (Lk. 3:22;4:1; Acts 10:38).

18. He who made all things also wills to sum up all things in Him (Eph. 1:10) so that God may be everything to everyone (1 Cor. 15:28). He sent his son who humbled Himself and became obedient unto death, even death on the cross (Phil. 2:8) in order that through the Son, we might be saved Land delivered from the dominion of darkness (Col. 1:13). Through the Son, we might be liberated from slavery in which sin has subjected us: hunger,

misery, oppression, ignorance, injustice and hatred, all of which originate from human selfishness; and that his Son, might reconcile the world to Himself (II Cor.5:19).

V. Areas of Mission

A. Worship

19. Worship is the offering of our total self to God in Christ that involves participation in the proclamation of the Life, Death and Resurrection and the Second Coming of Christ to the end that faith may be awakened and made alive in all men. It is *kerygma* in action and must be the spontaneous outcome of the "new life" in Christ as experienced in the breaking of the bread (Eucharist) and the fellowship of sharing (*koinonia*).

20. The Sacred Liturgy is the proclamation of the whole drama of Redemption from the Fall to the Incarnation: the Cross, Resurrection, Ascension and Second Coming of Christ. "For as often as you eat of this bread and drink the cup, you proclaim the Lord's Death until he comes" (I Cor. 11:26).

21. It is the nature of the Church to "declare the wonderful deeds if Him who called you out from darkness into His marvelous light" (I Peter 2-9). At the same time, an essential task of missionary activity is to plant and nurture the Church where she has not yet taken root. The chief means of implementation is the proclamation in word and deed of the Gospel of Jesus Christ and nourishing it with His body and Blood in the Eucharist.

22. In order to carry out and fulfill its task of evangelization, the Church (IFI) must seriously consider the joys, anxieties, aspirations, grievances and sufferings of humankind. It behooves the IFI to scrutinize the signs of the times and interpret them in the light of the Gospel, so that she can respond (mission) to the questionings of humankind and make present the saving work of God by her charity, service (*diakonia*) and solidarity to the world, especially to the poor, the oppressed and those in any way afflicted.

23. In her task of evangelization, the Church has to educate, especially those who have more than enough, that they may learn to share with the poor (Deut. 15:7-11,14-15; Job

29:16; Prov. 14:31; 19:17) what God has bestowed upon them (Prov. 22:22; I Sam. 30:24; Lk. 3:11; II Tim 2:6; Heb. 13:16) until misery exists no more (Deut. 15:4). After all, the problems of poverty, oppression and affliction are direct results of greed in all its forms.

24. Evangelization also serves to show Christ who saves through His Death and Resurrection (Acts 2:23-24;3:13-15) to men and women so that they be born anew (Jn. 3:7) and confess Christ as Lord and Savior (Rom. 10:9).

B. Human Development

25. The Church missionary presence in the world is her being the Salt, the Light, the Leaven (Mt. 5:13-15), in the same presence and manner that "they may have life and have it abundantly." (Jn. 10:10b).

26. Human development of people by the Word of God is nourishing them with His Body and Blood in the Eucharist; to develop the potentialities God has bestowed upon them; to enjoy the new life in Christ and have it abundantly; and, to enable them to share such abundance with their fellow beings.

27. It is therefore an essential missionary task of the Church to promote the good of everyone, of the whole person and of the whole human community that they may grow into "mature [personhood] in Christ" (Eph. 4:13). This concern for human development is an expression of our faith. We believe that [our] humanity is God's gift and it is our responsibility to God to preserve and uphold it. In the minds of the founding fathers of the IFI, concern for human development has always been there. Their cry and struggle were for liberation from the bondage of colonialism slavery, oppression, degradation, injustice, human indignity and dependence. The IFI, as an act of loyalty and remembrance, must carry on with passionate zeal that aspiration her founders had and for which they offered their lives. She can only continue this if she remains not being of this world even as Christ her Lord was not of the world (Jn. 17:16). Her security and kingdom is not with any socioeconomic and political institution but with God. However, let it not be forgotten

that the proclamation of the IFI was through the group of laborers led by Don Isabelo de los Reyes, Sr., the Father of Philippine labor movement.

28. As the Church is the universal sacrament of salvation, she has to continually effect and bring forth the abundance of that new life. This entails:

    a. The celebration of the Eucharist, in which the bond between God and [humankind] is effectively recalled and proclaimed, also demands commitment to justice, freedom and truth;

    b. The progressive elimination of hunger, disease and physical deprivation which suppress human freedom;

    c. Solidarity with the poor and the oppressed as an act of active obedience to Christ; and

    d. The progressive transformation of society by the power of the Gospel and the conversion of people to Christ.

C. Social Action

29. Social action is an activity inherent to the Church's calling. It is sending out in the service of the Kingdom of God to promote an atmosphere where people can enjoy a bigger share of the gifts of civilization for the development and fulfillment of their potentials as human beings.

30. Social action is a pastoral activity of the Church. The IFI will always be one with groups, organizations and communities that promote the welfare of people and of the human community, and the building up of the Kingdom of God. Thus the IFI stresses the importance of Christian education to encourage and educate believers, that they may grow to "mature [personhood], to the measure of the stature of the fullness of Christ, so that they may no longer be children tossed to and fro and carried about with every wind of doctrine..." (Eph. 4:13-15).

31. In pure pastoral activity we do not equate or confuse temporal progress in the Kingdom of God. Nevertheless, the former "to the extent that it can contribute to the better ordering of human society" is vital to the Kingdom

of God. The IFI has always been loyal to the cause of Her founding Fathers in promoting the welfare and dignity of the common [person], especially the laborer. She must, in all times and in all places, extend her pastoral ministry to workers and laborers with whom she was identified since the beginning. This demands the organization of a social action institution to carry this out.

D. Ecumenical Life

32. We believe that there is only One Body of Christ with Himself as the Foundation, i.e., the Church. It confesses One Lord, One Faith, One Baptism, One God and Father of us all, who is above all and through all and in all (Eph. 4:5-6).

33. It is in this oneness that we confess, affirm and seek to establish and renew the unity of the Church: unity in faith under the Fatherhood of God who reveals Himself in Jesus Christ and who continues to call us into the unity by the power of the Holy Spirit. At the same time we respect with humility the diversity of beliefs and practices of different religious faiths. We believe these different religious belief and practices are part of human life and therefore should be given due respect.

34. We treat these diversities with respect and acknowledge our unity in diversity in seeking to discern the realm of God and the workings of the Holy Spirit here and forever. We hold to that unity which Christ prayed for "that they may all be one; even as thou, Father, art in me, and I in thee, that they may also be in us..."(Jn. 17:21). These diversities with their consequent questions shed a new life and light in the understanding of the Church's teaching to make them understandable and thereby fortify the faithful. "When this the Church withdrew from the Roman Catholic Church, it repudiated the authority of the Pope and such doctrines, customs, and practices as were inconsistent with the Word of God, sound learning and good conscience. It did not intend to depart from Catholic doctrines, practices and disciplines as set by the council of the undivided Church. Departures that occurred were due to exigencies of the

times, and are to be corrected by official action so that this Church may be brought to the stream of historic Christianity and universally acknowledged as a true branch of the Catholic Church". (Art. of Religion #17)

35. We shall be one in witness with those whom we promote the Reign of God, the Reign of Love, Peace, Justice, Freedom and Truth. Opportunity is to be sought for closer cooperation with other branches of the Catholic Church and cordial relations shall be maintained with all who acknowledge Jesus Christ as Lord and Savior.

E. Renewal and Reconciliation

36. "Renewal and reform of the Church are necessary because the Church consists first, of human beings, and second, of sinful human beings". Though she can be described as" not having spot of wrinkle, holy and without blemish (Eph. 5:27)", yet she is never finished and complete. In her pilgrimage, she is always beset with crises, which not only threaten her unity but also deform her.

37. As one doctor of the Church said, "whenever in my books I have described the Church as being without spot or wrinkle, it is understood that she is already, but she is preparing herself to be so when she too will appear in glory. For in the present, because of ignorance and weakness in her members, she must confess afresh each day 'Forgive us our trespasses".

38. That the Church may be glorious, without spot or wrinkle, is the final goal to which we are leading through the passion of Christ. It will be also only in our eternal home, not in our journey there during which if we said we had no sin, we are deceiving ourselves, as we are told in the First Epistle of John.

39. In so far as she is deformed, she has to be reformed. The Church has to continually renew herself, giving herself a new form, a new shape in history, adopting a new order to make the Gospel alive to all men.

40. The present demands that the IFI develop new forms of liturgy in order that her life may be renewed and made alive.

41. In the light of the questionings of [humankind] and the emerging aspirations of [all], she has to rethink and renew her teachings.
42. In the midst of sinful humanity, she is called and sent by God to be the agent of reconciliation (II Cor. 5:18-19). God first reconciled her to Him, "in his body of flesh and death, in order to present you holy and blameless and irreproachable before him," "to make expiation for the sins of the people" (Heb. 2:17).
43. Our reconciliation with those who are separated from us is based on the fact that God in Christ first reconciled us to Himself. It is our sorrow that many of our people have left the IFI, and it is with humility and repentance that we shall seek the reconciliation of all. "We do not wish to put anyone in history on trial; we shall not seek to establish who was right and who was wrong. Responsibility is divided. We want only to say, "let us come together, let is unmake and undo our divisions".

Appendix E

Aglipayan Ministry

Koinonia is the life of the Triune God from which proceeds the communitarian dimension and dynamism of the *Iglesia Filipina Independiente*. *Koinonia* inspires the *Iglesia Filipina Independiente* to the vocation of *diakonia*. *Koinonia*, which is fellowship, and *diakonia*, which is service, is our ministry rooted in the words and works of Jesus Christ.

Jesus is the source, medium and message of our ministry. Jesus, as the Scriptures attest, is foremost a prophet in the tradition of the Old Testament. Heir to this tradition, he 'lived in the midst of his people' (John 1.14) sharing their pains, anxieties and hopes; as a testimony to his liberating love for his people 'he offered his life' (John 15.13) for them.

Jesus the Prophet announced the Reign of God, not only consoling, but challenging the people to surrender themselves to the requisites of its presence and power in history and human situation. Jesus proclaimed the Reign of God 'bringing good news to the poor, liberty to the captives, recovery of sight to the blind, setting the oppressed free and announcing the year of the Lord's favor' (Luke 4.16-19).

The *Iglesia Filipina Independiente*, professing and proclaiming faith in Jesus, affirms her pastoral and prophetic ministry to all People of God in a situation of socio-economic and socio-political crises arising from a semi-colonial and semi-feudal frameworks operating in the country. She shows concerns and commits herself to the plight of the poor whose fields have been added to another field to constitute one hacienda, whose houses have been joined with another house to become homeless wanderers and unemployed in the streets (Isaiah 5.8). She shows concerns and commits herself to the predicament of the righteous who are sold for a silver and the needy for a pair of shoes, the poor who are trampled at the head into the dust of the earth, and the maiden whom a man and his father went into (Amos 2.8)

The *Iglesia Filipina Independiente* cries out against who possess power but perverse the poor of our land. She calls all to do what the Lord requires; to do justice, and to love mercy and to walk humbly with God (Micah 6.8), and to observe the weightier matters of the law; justice, mercy and faith (Matthew 23.23).

Jesus entrusted his ministry to the *ekklesia*. Jesus tells his disciples, 'Go and preach, 'The Reign of God is near! Heal the sick, raise the dead, cleanse the leprous and drive out demons' (Matthew 10.8). The *Iglesia Filipina Independiente* submits herself to this mandate of servanthood to the people, especially to the poor. Jesus associates the Reign of God, not with the salvation of souls, but with the restoration of the well-beingness and wholeness of the human person. Our ministry affirms the well-beingness and wholeness of the human person, thus our advocacy for the basic rights of the peasants and workers.

Our ministry is consistent with its solidarity with our brothers and sisters who are marginalized and made poor by systems that nurture oppression. The *Iglesia Filipina Independiente* is conceived through the advocacy and aspiration of the people to liberate themselves from slavery for hundreds of years. The present socio-economic and socio-political maladies stemming from half a millennium of foreign political control and landlessness, compel the *Iglesia Filipina Independiente* more than ever to live out her national and democratic heritage and her ministry of koinonia and diakonia, that the People of God may experience Jesus offer of an 'abundant life' (John 10.10).

Our ministry is for the service of the Reign of God. Our ministry is rooted in spirituality, nonetheless, not the spirituality that is passive asceticism, rather the spirituality that proceeds from an animated anticipation of the Reign of God. Our spirituality is what leads us to the progressive ministry of renewing the human person and of rebuilding the human community. The *Iglesia Filipina Independiente* carries out her ministry in the guidance of the Spirit of God who anointed Jesus 'to proclaim the good news to the poor' (Luke 4.16). It is the one Spirit of God that is inspiring and inciting her to commit herself to the coming of the Reign of God.

We, your bishops and Priests, acknowledge our ministry as your servants in the *Iglesia Filipina Independiente*, for even he who leads us to liberation and life comes 'not to be served but to serve' (Mark 10.45). We rejoice in God for calling and consecrating us into this vocation, and yet, we recognize and remorse over our frailties and failures. We humbly confess before God, and to you, God's People, of our sinfulness, unworthiness and unfaithfulness, and we ask you to pray for us that despite our weakness we may continue to witness to the life giving and liberating love of Jesus, our Lord and Liberator.

Today, brothers and sisters, we renew our commitment to the ministry of Jesus, the Prophet, to the ministry of koinonia and diakonia; and as we pray for the Spirit of God to renew our nation and the whole of creation, we also pray to Him to recreate in us, and in all of us, chaste and clean hearts.

Appendix F

Aglipayan Statement on the Local Church

The *Iglesia Filipina Independiente*, as an ecclesial community, manifests, represents and realizes in almost every place and every time the One and Universal Church of Christ and witnesses to Jesus, her Lord and Liberator, through the exercise of mission and ministry of the local churches – the dioceses. These local churches, entrusted with the proclamation of the Word and the celebration of the Sacraments, bear the fullness of the *Iglesia Filipina Independiente.*

The local churches or dioceses exist in ecclesial communion that no individual local church can claim autonomy and independence, but only nurturing interrelatedness, mutual responsibility and interdependence with other local churches. This dynamism arises from the actuality and verity that all local churches, profess and proclaim the one and the same faith; receive and preach the same Gospel; are sanctified by the one and the same baptism and nurtured by the one and the same Eucharist; and are served by a common ministry. All local churches are subject to the grace of one and the same Father, have one and the same Lord, and are inspired by one and the same Holy Spirit. This communion is expressed in service and witness to the world; and is sustained by a fundamental coherence and consonance in the living elements of apostolicity and unity: the baptism and Eucharist, the Nicene and Apostles' creeds, the ordered ministry and the canon of Scriptures. These living elements found at the local churches serve to ensure the fidelity and authentic succession of the IFI to the apostolic faith and mission. Thus, the local church, however, poor and small, incarnates and actualizes the fullness of the one and universal Church of Christ.

Bishops, collegially sharing the ministry of oversight in the *Iglesia Filipina Independiente* with the primacy of the *Obispo Máximo*, bear the fullness of ministry and serve the unity, continuity and communion of the local churches. The bishops, who head the local churches, are the principal dispensers of the Sacrament of Orders, and from whom both priests and deacons derive their authority in ministry.

Bishops exercise the ministry of oversight in personal, collegial and communal ways. Their specific ministry however is exercised responsibly in partnership with other bishops, clergy and laity of the whole *Iglesia Filipina Independiente*. This interdependence in the exercise of ministry is an expression of the fundamental unity in the life of the Triune God – the Father, Son and Holy Spirit. Thus, episcopal ministry is not authoritarian ministry, but rather a ministry that is exercised in service to the ecclesial community. The episcopal ministry is of fundamental importance in the life of the local and universal Church, being the ministry of pastoring and building up God's people. It reflects the communion of the Father, Son and Holy Spirit, and from whom we draw order in the life of the Church.

Our reaffirmation of the local churches enables us to define the diocese as the locus of the mission and ministry of the *Iglesia Filipina Independiente*, and to rediscover the prominence of episcopal ministry in our Church, whom, together with the ministry of all our clergy and laity, bears witness to our Catholic and Apostolic faith.

Appendix G

Aglipayan Stance Toward LGBTIQ+ Persons

In February 2017, the Aglipayan church released the following statement on its stance toward members of the LGBTIQ+ community.

Our Common Humanity, Our Shared Dignity

"In Christ Jesus, you are all children of God through faith."
—Galatians 3:26

As we gathered to study and pray, we, the Supreme Council of Bishops of the *Iglesia Filipina Independiente*, strived to find unity in our Christian faith and to discover new ways to make the Church more reflective of God's universal, unconditional love; more reflective of the nurturing and complementing diversity within the mystery of the Triune God.

The Church's vocation is to live out God's boundless truth (Acts 13:47); her mission to make the world a more just and joyous place for all (Isaiah 1:17). Constantly needing renewal, the Church always works to reform herself through the inspiration of God's Spirit, so as to enable herself in a more effective way in bringing the Gospel of Christ to its own communities and the wider society.

Faithfulness to God's mission requires that sincere efforts be made to see that justice is done for God's people as the *Iglesia Filipina Independiente* engages herself in and confronts the challenges of our present generation. Enlightened by the Scriptures, the Church has been vigilant against unjust systems, confronting racism, slavery and sexism within and without, in a continuous process of theological reflection and pastoral engagement. Continually following the Spirit's inspiration in history, our Church has joyfully affirmed the gift of women priesthood as part of the life-giving mission of Christ three decades ago.

Now, we are confronted by the universal challenge to stand on individuals who are lesbian, gay, bisexual, transgender, intersex, queer/questioning and who identify with the other sexual minorities, also known as LGBTIQ+.

We believe that the Church must openly embrace God's people of all sexes, sexual orientations, gender identities and expressions (SSOGIE) as we embark on a journey toward a just and peaceful world. God's love and compassion, and the core message of peace and justice in Jesus' life, lead us in taking this humble step to give objective recognition to LGBTIQ+ individuals, and promote their dignity and rights as human persons.

Seeking to incarnate the rich message and meaning of God's Word in our generation, the Church upholds the revolutionary reading of the Scriptures as she endeavors to keep herself unstained from the world (James 1:27) and worldly prejudices (James 4:12). We uphold the rich treasure of human sexuality being brought to light in our present generation.

Thus, we reaffirm our commitment to proclaim the Gospel to all the world so that people, of all SSOGIE, may receive God's grace through faith in Christ (Galatians 3:26-29). Conforming to God's design for His grace to freely flow to all people, we hope to break down the walls of stigma and prejudice within the Church.

Our Church proclaims the universality of God's love. Our God is love (1 John 4:8;16), not hate and hostility; and love is a mighty force (1 Corinthians 13:13). We follow the footsteps of Jesus, who embraced all people with equal love, respect and compassion (Luke 4:18-19) and who extended his friendship to LGBTIQ+ individuals (Matthew 8:5-13).

We recognize and rejoice in the presence of the LGBTIQ+ community amongst us. We applaud their persistent belief in God's embracing love. The judgment, intolerance and non-acceptance have not stopped many from serving the Church, even through the priestly order. They have enriched the life, work and witness of the *Iglesia Filipina Independiente*.

We humbly ask for forgiveness for the many times we have shown indifference, and have made the LGBTIQ+ people feel less human, discriminated against and stigmatized. We apologize for instances they felt that, through our thoughts, words and deeds, God's love is selective.

The Gospel teaches us to live in love (Ephesians 5:2), to live out love (1 John 3:18), to offer love to each other (John 13:34). It instructs us to love God through the oppressed (Matthew 25: 34-40); to love other people as we would ourselves (Hebrew 13:1-3). We are told to cast out fear with perfect love (1 John 4:18). The greatest expression of love is liberation (James 1:25), especially for the *Iglesia Filipina Independiente*, who was given birth by the Filipino people's struggle against historical injustice and inequality. We steadfastly hold on to our historic heritage in proclaiming Jesus' message for the marginalized.

We offer our Church as a community where LGBTIQ+ people can freely and responsibly express themselves. With them, we pronounce God's all-inclusive love. Being God's children, LGBTIQ+ individuals are imbued with God's gift of human dignity. The discrimination against them is part of the struggle for human rights. The Church affirms that LGBTIQ+ individuals have all the right to love and be loved, and commits to offer them opportunities to realize their full potential and dignity as human persons, as God's children.

LGBTIQ+ individuals are called to give witness to our faith through living an exemplary Christian life. To become bearers of God's compassion and charity in the world, they are exhorted by the Church, as all faithful, to abide by Article of Religion 12: "Holiness, altruism, obedience to God's Commandments, and a zeal for His honor and glory are incumbent upon Clergy and Laity alike, therefore all should be trained in a clean and disciplined life, not neglecting prayer, study, and the exercise of moral discipline."

The *Iglesia Filipina Independiente* offers herself as a welcoming Church for LGBTIQ+ persons. We commit our local churches and communities to LGBTIQ+-affirming ministries. We celebrate God's grace through the Sacraments, and are grateful for God who does not discriminate anyone from receiving His grace in the Sacraments.

We believe God's love is both encompassing and supreme, and that we must strive to share the same to the world. We pray for God to make the Church a continuing testament of his motherly love (Matthew 23:37). We, your bishops, offer our hands and warm embrace in Christian friendship (John 15:13) to LGBTIQ+ persons, so they may celebrate their gifts and calling, and fully and responsibly express themselves through the *Iglesia Filipina Independiente*.

We hope this move can effect change among Churches and church people. Through this declaration, we implore agenda-setters to discuss laws and initiatives challenging LGBTIQ+ discrimination. Only through this can we truly protect our brothers and sisters in the community, against issues such as abuse and the rise in HIV and AIDS cases in the sector; against avoidable fear, suffering and caution.

Our collective existence as human beings, our shared aspiration and struggle for a just and peaceful world, our common humanity, tell us that we are not at all different from LGBTIQ+ persons.

With this statement, we publish a prayer for equality:

> Our Creator God, who intended the diversity of Creation, we come to you now with all humility. In your image, you blessed us with equal dignity, but we've imposed our own inequalities. We have scarred your Order, in which all are free, in which all matter despite sex, sexual orientation, gender identity and expression. Allow us to see beyond our persistent traditions and biases; our hurtful hate and suspicion. May we see your vision, where all are equal in the pursuit of your abundant blessings. Reveal to us our common humanity, our shared dignity; make crumble our many walls with our united wills. Send us with passion and strength to mend the world divided, so that it may transform into your unified reign of peace based on justice. All this we seek in the name of Jesus Christ, our Lord and Savior. Amen.

Rt. Rev. Antonio Ablon
Secretary
Supreme Council of Bishops

Rt. Rev. Rhee Timbang
Chairperson
Supreme Council of Bishops

Most Rev. Ephraim Fajutagana
Obispo Máximo
Iglesia Filipina Independiente

Appendix H

Prominent Aglipayans

The following prominent Aglipayans are listed by year of birth.

- **Melchora Aquino de Ramos** (1812-1919), the Filipina revolutionary known as *Tandang Sora* ("Elder Sora") due to her age during the 1896 Philippine Revolution. Known as the "Grand Woman of the Revolution" and "Mother of Balintawak," she was one of the most prominent and devoted Aglipayans in Caloocan, Manila.

- **Felipe Siojo Buencamino, Sr.** (1848-1929), the Filipino composer, member of the Malolos Congress, co-author of the Constitution of the Philippine Republic at Malolos, and a co-founder of the PIC.

- **Ladislao Bonus** (1854-1908), the composer, conductor and bass player known as the "Father of the Filipino opera."

- **Apolinario Mabini y Maranan** (1864-1903), the Filipino political philosopher and revolutionary who wrote a constitutional plan for the First Philippine Republic and served as the first Prime Minister of the Philippines in 1899.

- **Baldomero Aguinaldo y Baloy** (1869-1915), a revolutionary general and first cousin of General Emilio Aguinaldo, who served as President of the PIC *Comité de Caballeros* (Men's Committee) and was the grandfather of Philippine Prime Minister César Virata.

- **Emilio Aguinaldo y Famy** (1869-1964), the first President of the Philippines, who, along with other , together with other Caviteño revolutionary generals and officers, cleared the way for Cavite to be a stronghold of the PIC. His wife, Hilaria del Rosario, his mother, Trinidad Famy, and his youngest sister, Felicidad, served as officers of the PIC's *Comisión de Damas* (Women's Commission).

- **Aurelio Tolentino y Valenzuela** (1869-1915), a prominent Pampango writer, dramatist, and co-founder of the Katipunan, who helped establish the Aglipayan church in Pampanga.

- **Vicente Sotto** (1877-1950), a dramatist, anti-friar writer and journalist, and fiery publisher/editor of *Ang Suga* and *El Pueblo*, he helped found the PIC in Cebu.

- **Lope K. Santos** (1879-1963), nationalist playwright who introduced the now-obsolete *Abakada Tagalog* spelling reform in 1940.

- **Mariano Marcos y Rubio** (1897-1945), a lawyer and Congressman (1925-1931), best-known as the father of former president and dictator Ferdinand Marcos.

- **José Garvida Flores** (1900-1944), patriot and prolific Ilokano writer and playwright who composed *"Filipinas Nadayag a Filipinas"* ("Philippines, Beloved Philippines"), which is sung at PIC services.

- **Calixto Oriola Zaldívar** (1904-1979), father of Enrique Zaldívar and Salvación Zaldívar-Pérez, he served as Governor of Antique (1951-1955) and Associate Justice of the Supreme Court (1964-1974), he served as president of the PIC's National Lay Organization.

- **Gedeón G. Quijano** (1910-1989), the son of former PIC Bishop Juan P. Quijano, he served as Governor of Misamis Occidental (1946-1967).

- **Ferdinand Emmanuel Edralín Marcos, Sr.** (1917-1989), son of Mariano Marcos, he served as President of the Philippines (1965-1986) and converted to Roman Catholicism to marry Imelda R. Marcos.

- **Gardeopatra G. Quijano** (1918-2003), Visayan dentist and teacher regarded as the first Cebuana feminist fiction writer, she served as President of WOPIC (Women of the Philippine Independent Church, 1975-1977).

- **César Virata** (1930-), business leader, technocrat, Finance Minister (1970-1986) and fourth Prime Minister of the Philippines (1981-1986), he was the grandnephew of the first Philippine President, Emilio Aguinaldo.

- **Crispin Beltrán** (1933-2008), Congressman of the Toiling Masses Party and "Grand Old Man of Philippine Labor," a staunch critic of President Gloria Macapagal-Arroyo and famously imprisoned in 2006-2007 on disputed charges of rebellion and sedition.
- **Benjamín Abalos, Sr**. (1935-), Former mayor of Mandaluyong (1988-1998), former Chair of the Commission on Elections and the Metropolitan Manila Development Authority, and father of Benhur "Benjamín" de Castro Abalos Jr.
- **Roy Agullana Cimatu** (1946-), 29th Chief of Staff of the Philippine Armed Forces, former Special Envoy to the Middle East, and current Philippine Secretary of Environment & Natural Resources.
- **Bayani Flores Fernando** (1946-), former Chair of the Metropolitan Manila Development Authority.
- **Daniel Fernando** (1962-), Governor of Bulacan (2019-).
- **Benhur "Benjamín" de Castro Abalos Jr.** (1962-), son of former mayor of Mandaluyong Benjamín Abalos, Sr., former mayor of Mandaluyong (1998-2016), husband of current Mandaluyong mayor Carmelita "Menchie" Aguilar Abalos.
- **Carmelita "Menchie" Aguilar Abalos** (1962-), mayor of Mandaluyong (2016-), succeeding her husband, Benhur Abalos.
- **Rhodora Javier Cadiao** (unk.), Governor of Antique (2015-).
- **Eduardo Firmalo y Chang** (unk.), former Governor of Romblon (2010-2019).
- **Deo Macalma** (unk.), Philippine anchorman for the nation's oldest radio station, and mayor of Star City.
- **Enrique A. Zaldívar** (unk.), the son of Justice Calixto Zaldívar and brother of future Antique Governor Salvación Zaldívar-Pérez, he served as Governor of Antique (1980-1984) and Ambassador to Brunei.
- **Salvación Zaldívar-Pérez** (unk.), the daughter of Justice Calixto Zaldívar and sister of Antique Governor Enrique Zaldívar, she served as Governor of Antique (2001-2010).

Appendix I

Significant Aglipayan Churches

Dr. Valiant O. Dayagbil writes that "the Filipino Church" is used to designate a number of churches with similar polity, and that the name "Philippine Independent Church" or "Philippine Independent Catholic Church" serves as an "umbrella" term for "a conglomeration of churches, an organic union, so to speak." Here is a listing of the various Philippine Independent Catholic churches arising after the start of the 20th century, with the names of their founder and/or leaders. Several of these are listed in *Philippine Studies*, Vol. 16, no. 1 (1968), where Jesuit Fathers Pedro de Achútegui and Florentino Cuenquis wrote, "since 1955, the term 'Aglipayan' has become a generic name which can be applied to many distinct churches."

1902 - *Iglesia Filipina Independiente* (IFI)
(Philippine Independent Church, PIC)
President Pascual Poblete; Secretary Isabelo de los Reyes, Sr.;
Supreme Bishop Gregorio Aglípay & successors

1904 - *Iglesia de la Libertad* (IL)
Gen. Baldomero Aguinaldo (brother of President Emilio Aguinaldo)
* A revival of the *Iglesia Filipina Independiente de Binakayan* in Cavite,
the church was later absorbed into the PIC
* Succeeded again in 1938 and was registered by Bishop José Gamad

1920s - *Iglesia Filipina Reformada* (IFR)
(Philippine Reformed Church)
Ángel Flor Mata
* Dissolved when leaders returned to the Roman church in 1929

1924 - *Iglesia Filipina Evangélica Independiente*
(Independent Philippine Evangelical Church)
Supreme Bishop Demetrio Pascual
Bishop Ciriaco de las Llagas is also credited for this church

September 24, 1928 - Filipino Christian Church (FCC)
Bishop Ciriaco de las Llagas, at Dolores, Tayabas
* In 1962, at the death of de las Llagas, they had 14 ministers

October 11, 1930 - *Iglesia Filipina Liberal*
Philippine Liberal Church (PLC)
Bishop Ceferino Ramírez, founder, seceded from the PIC
* The church was later led by Bishop Vicente Vergara

1930 - *Iglesia Católica Apóstolica Nacional* **(ICAN),**
Rev. David A. Romero
* Broke from the PIC on January 12, 1930, in Muñoz, Nueva Ecija
* During the 1944 Japanese occupation, the ICAN had 50,000 members

April 1939 – [The Trinitarian, de los Reyes Faction of the PIC]
Bishop Isabelo de los Reyes, Jr.
* He won sole rights to the PIC name, properties & assets in 1955

1947 - *Iglesia Cismática Filipina Nacional* **(ICFN)**
Bishop Camilo Diel
* In 1956, the ICFN had 10,000 people in 40 organized & 10 unorganized
communities, served by 14 full-time & 6 part-time ministers

1951 - Bishop's Church
Bishop José Pasión, in Umingan, Pangasinan

1946 - Independent Church of Filipino Christians (ICFC)
[The Unitarian, Fonacier Faction of the PIC, a.k.a., "Filipinistas"]
Bishop Santiago Fonacier, then Bishop Ramón Abaya y Sisón
* Registered in 1955, after defeat at the Supreme Court
* Reunited with the PIC on March 24, 1974

1958 - Christ Jesus' Holy Church (CJHC) – Unitarian
Bishop Pedro Aglípay, formerly of the Philippine Unitarian Church
* A sole corporation with the Securities & Exchange Commission

July 3, 1966 - *Iglesia Católica Apóstolica Filipina Independiente*
Holy Catholic Apostolic Christian Church (HCAC)

Before 1968 - Church of God (CG)
a.k.a., the Catholic and Apostolic Aglipayan Memorial Church
Rev. Felipe Yezaya, in Bansud, Mindoro Oriental
* They had a single registered minister

Before 1968 - *Iglesia Nacional de Filipinas* **(INF)**
Bishop Solomón Elegado,
then Rev. Proceso Reyes of Sampaloc, Manila (formerly of the PIC)
* They had nine ministers

1955 - Philippine Unitarian Church (PUC)
A Unitarian church by Bishop Pedro Aglípay,
then Bishop Ángel Bitanga
* Comprised of former members of Fonacier's PIC faction
* Its motto: "Be a Unitarian to be a true Aglipayan"

1987 - *Iglesia Catolica Filipina Independiente*
(Philippine Independent Catholic Church)
Former PIC Supreme Bishop Macario Ga
* Reconciled with the PIC on February 4, 1994

The following churches are mentioned by Dr. Valiant O. Dayagbil:

Iglesia Aglipayana - Unknown date
(Aglipayan Church)

Iglesia Católica Aglipayana - Unknown date
(Aglipayan Catholic Church)

Iglesia Independiente Aglipayana - Unknown date
(Aglipayan Independent Church)

Appendix J

Aglipayan Bibliography

Aglípay, G. (1903, October 29). The Independent Catholic Church in the Philippines. *The Independent*, 55(2865), 2571-2575.

Aglípay, G. (1904, April 28). The Aglipayan Schism in the Philippines. *The Independent* (New York), *56*(2891), 953-957.

Aglípay, G. (1905). *Catecismo de la Iglesia Filipina Independiente*. Manila: Fajardo y Compañía. bit.ly/3k96MkM.

Aglípay, G. (1908). *[Carta de] Obispado Máximo de Filipinas. Independiente para el Año Bisiesto del Señor*. Barcelona: A. Virgili.

Aglípay, G. (1925). *Pagasisiyam sa Virgen sa Balintawak — Ang Virgen sa Balintawak ay ang Inang Bayan*. Manila.

Aglípay, G. (1926). *Novenary of the Motherland — The Motherland is Symbolized in the Envisioned Mother of Balintawak*. Manila. bit.ly/3554RaL.

Aglípay, G. (1929). *Al Padre de Todos: Libro de Oraciones y Enseñanzas de la Iglesia Filipina Independiente*. Manila.

Alip, E.M. (1941, October). Aglipayanism: A Critical Exposition. *Unitas*, *20*(3), 385-392.

Alipit, R. (1962, July). The Position of the Philippine Independent Church. *Southeast Asia Journal of Theology*, 4(1), 32-36.

Belén de Lara, G. (1930). *Ang Paghihimagsik ni Obispo Aglipay*. Manila.

Binsted, N.S. (1957, November). *Iglesia Filipina Independiente*. Manila.

Binsted, N.S. (1958). The Philippine Independent Church (Iglesia Filipina Independiente). *Historical Magazine of the Protestant Episcopal Church*, *7*, 209-246. [This is the reprint of his 1957 article.]

Boonen, M. (1929). Le Schisme Aglipayen. *Compte-rendu de la Septième Semaine Missiologie de Louvain*. Louvain.

Bowers, G.B. (1922, May). Animism, Aglipay's Cult and Christianity's Eclipse in the Philippines. *Open Court*, *36*(5), 300-309.

Brand, D.V. (1980). *The Philippine Independent Church: A Social Movement*. Unpublished Ph.D. thesis, Ithaca: Cornell University.

Cabillas, D.M. (2002, July). Iglesia Filipina Independiente (IFI): Comments from Churches Involved in Union Negotiations. *The Ecumenical Review, 54*(3).

Chandlee, H.E. (1954, October). The Philippine Independent Church. *Pan-Anglican, 5,* 22-26.

Clifford, M.D. (1960). *Aglipayanism as a Political Movement.* Unpublished Ph.D. dissertation, St. Louis University, St. Louis, Missouri.

Clifford, M.D. (1969). Iglesia Filipina Independiente: The Revolutionary Church. In Anderson, G.H. (Ed.) *Studies in Philippine Church History.* Ithaca: Cornell University Press, 223-255.

Clymer, K.J. (1978, December). The Methodist Response to Philippine Nationalism, 1899-1916. *Church History, 47*(4), 421-433.

Coleman, A. (1905, April). The Inside of the Aglipayan Church. *The American Catholic Quarterly Review, 30*(118), 368-381.

Conde-Bebis, K. (2009). Youth of the Iglesia Filipina Independiente: A Historical Journey. bit.ly/3k5ahZL.

Constantino, R. (1985). Documents, Nationalism and the Hero from Batac. *Journal of Contemporary Asia, 15*(1), 117-128.

Cornish, L.C. (1942). *The Philippines Calling.* Philadelphia: Dorrance & Company.

Cruz, R.V. (1961, June). The Founding of the Aglipayan Church. *Philippine Social Science and Humanities Review, 26*(2), 187-212.

Dayagbil, V.O. (n.d.). The Philippine Independent Catholic Church: A Brief History. bit.ly/353C1Yl.

de Achútegui, P.S. (1978). Gregorio Aglipay: The Rebel Priest, *Filipino Heritage, 9,* 2326-2330.

de Achútegui, P.S. & Bernad, M.A. (1960). *Religious Revolution in the Philippines* (4 volumes). Manila: Ateneo de Manila.

de Achútegui, P.S. & Bernad, M.A. (1960). Brent, Herzog, Morayta and Aglipay. *Philippine Studies 8*(3), 568-583.

de Archutegui, P.S. & Bernad, M.A. (1964, July). The Aglipayan Churches and the Census of 1960. *Philippine Studies, 12*(3), 446-459.

de Boer, W.H. & Smit, P.B. (2008). Die frühen Beziehungen zwischen der Iglesia Filipina Independiente und den altkatholischen Kirchen der Utrechter Union [The Early Relationships Between the Iglesia Filipina Independiente and the Old Catholic Churches of the Union of Utrecht], *Internationale Kirchliche Zeitschrift*, *98*, 122-144, 169-190.

de Boer, W.H. (2012). *In necessariis unitas. Hintergründe zu den ökumenischen Beziehungen zwischen der Iglesia Filipina Independiente, den Kirchen der Anglikanischen Gemeinschaft und den altkatholischen Kirchen der Utrechter Union [In necessariis unitas. On the Background of the Ecumenical Relationships Between the Iglesia Filipina Independiente, the Churches of the Anglican Communion and the Old Catholic Churches of the Union of Utrecht].* Frankfurt on the Main: Peter Lang.

de los Reyes, I. (1906). *Oficio Divino de la Iglesia Filipina Independiente.* Barcelona.

de los Reyes, I. (1908). *Biblia Filipina: Primera Piedra para un Génesis científico expuesto según las rectificaciones de Jesús.* Barcelona.

de los Reyes, I. (1908). *Calendario de la Iglesia Filipina Independiente para el año bisiesto del Señor, 1908.* Barcelona.

de los Reyes, I. (1906). *Oficio Divino de la Iglesia Filipina Independiente.* Barcelona: A. Virgili.

de los Reyes, I., Jr. (1948, June). The Iglesia Filipina Independiente (Philippine Independent Church): A Brief History. *Historical Magazine of the Protestant Episcopal Church, 17,* 132-137.

de los Reyes, I., Jr. (1956, April 11). Philippine Church Reborn. *Christian Century, 37,* 455-456.

de los Reyes, I., Jr. (1959, Fall). The Iglesia Filipina Independiente Today," *Pan-Anglican, 10,* 71-76.

Deats, R.L. (1965, April-June). Nationalism and the Churches in the Philippines. *Silliman Journal, 12*(2), 152-167.

Deats, R.L. (1967). *Nationalism and Christianity in the Philippines.* Dallas: Southern Methodist University Press.

Doeppers, D.F. (1976, April). The Philippine Revolution and the Geography of Schism. *Geographical Review, 66*(2), 158-177.

154

Doeppers, D.F. (1977, Third Quarter). Changing Patterns of Aglipayan Adherence in the Philippines, 1918-1970. *Philippine Studies, 25*, 265-277.

Dresse, V.A. (1927). *The Aglipayan Movement in the Philippine Islands.* M.A. Thesis. Indianapolis: College of Missions.

Fabella, G.F. (1960, December). Gregorio Aglipay in History. *Historical Bulletin*, 4(4), 27-35.

Fernández García, C. (1924). *La Doctrina de la Iglesia Filipina Independiente: Exposición y Crítica.* Manila.

Fonacier, S. (1952, September 1). *Proceedings of the Asamblea Magna of the Iglesia Filipina Independiente, Church of the Heroes and Martyrs.* Manila.

Fonacier, T.S. (1954). *Gregorio Aglipay y Labayán: A Short Biography.* Manila: McCullough.

Foronda, M.A. (1962, March). Rizal and Aglipay. *The Journal of History*, 10(1), 3-20.

Foronda, M.A. (1966, December 31). Rizal's Influence on Aglipay. *Chronicle Magazine, 21*(53), 3-20. [A reprint of Foronda's 1962 article]

Gealogo, F.A. (2011). Religion, Science, and *Bayan* in the *Iglesia Filipina Independiente.* In D..L. Woods (Ed.), From Wilderness to Nation: Interrogating *Bayan,.* Quezon City: University of the Philippines Press, 108-121.

Gealogo, F.A. (2010). Time, Identity, and Nation in the Aglipayan Novenario ng Balintawak and Calendariong Maanghang. *Philippine Studies 58*(1-2), 147-168.

Go, F.S. (1980). The Philippine Independent Church: Religious Conversion and the Spread of Aglipayanism in Cebu Province. *Philippine Quarterly of Culture and Society, 8*, 150-167.

Gowing, P.G. (1965, April-June). Christianity in the Philippines Yesterday and Today. *Silliman Journal, 12*(2), 109-151

Guevarra, R.C. (1968, April 29). How Aglipay Saved a Whole Town. *Examiner*, 307, 11 & 23.

Hermann, A. (2013). Transregional Contacts between Independent Catholic Churches in Asia around 1900: The Case of the Iglesia Filipina Independiente and the Independent Catholics of Ceylon. In C. Burlacioiu, & A. Hermann (Eds.), *Veränderte Landkarten. Auf dem Weg zu einer polyzentrischen Geschichte des Weltchristentums.*

Festschrift für Klaus Koschorke zum 65 (pp. 139-150). Wiesbaden: Harrassowitz.

Hermann, A. (2014). The Early Periodicals of the Iglesia Filipina Independiente (1903–1904) and the Emergence of a Transregional and Transcontinental Indigenous-Christian Public Sphere. *Philippine Studies, 62*(3–4), 549–565.

Hermann, A. (2014). Transnational Networks of Philippine Intellectuals and the Emergence of an Indigenous-Christian Public Sphere around 1900. In K. Koschorke, & A. Hermann (Eds.), Polycentric structures in the history of world Christianity: Studies in the History of Christianity in the Non-Western World / *Polyzentrische Strukturen in der Geschichte des Weltchristentums (Studien zur Außereuropäischen Christentumsgeschichte Asien, Africa, Lateinamerika)* (pp. 193-203). Wiesbaden: Harrassowitz.

Herzog, E. (1903, December 1). Letter to Gregorio Aglipay. Quezon City: St. Andrew's Theological Seminary IFI Archive, OM 1.1, 1903-1905, Box 1, Folder 1.

IFI History Committee (2011, June 8). Celebrating the Heritage for National Freedom, Independence and Abundant Life: A Historical Sketch. bit.ly/3lRu3Ip.

Iglesia Filipina Independiente (1925). *Calendario ng Iglesia Filipina. Manila.*

Lagasca, M. (1939). *Iglesia Filipina Independiente: Su Origen, Significación e Importancia.* Manila.

Lynch, D. (1913, January 11). A Defunct Religion. *America, 8*(14). 319-320.

Lynch, F. (1956). Aglipayanism. In Eggan, F., et al. (Eds.), *Area Handbook on the Philippines, 2,* Chicago, The University of Chicago Press, 687-717. bit.ly/37dK2g4.

Manaligod, A.M. (1977). *Gregorio Aglipay: Hero or Villain?* Manila: Communication Foundation for Asia.

McGavran, D.A. (1958, Summer). The Independent Church in the Philippines. *Encounter, 19*(3), 299-321.

Nebot, F. (1905). *La Doctrina de la Iglesia Filipino Independiente Comparada con la Doctrina de la Iglesia Catolica.* Manila.

156

Ochosa, O.A. (1969, May 24). Gregorio Aglipay: the Fighting Padre. *Mirror*, 10-11.

Ortega, J. (1947, October). El Bautismo en la Secta Aglipayana. *Boletín Eclesiástico*, 21.

Pargas, L.S. (1962). *The Filipino Nationalist Movement from 1900 to 1910*. M.A. thesis. Quezon City: University of the Philippines.

Parker, D.D. (1938, November). Church and State in the Philippines (1896-1906). *The Philippine Social Science Review, 10*(4), 354-371.

Poethig, R.P. (1967, First Quarter). The Philippine Independent Church: The Agony of Philippine Nationalism. *Silliman Journal, 14*(1), 27-54.

Ramírez, P. (1970), June-December). The Aglipay Story. *Ilocos Review, 2*(2), 159-170.

Ranche, A.M. (2000). The Iglesia Filipina Independiente (IFI): A People's Movement for National Freedom, Independence and Prosperity. *Philippiniana Sacra, 35*, 513-534.

Ranche, A.M. (n.d.). An Introduction to the Iglesia Filipina Independiente. bit.ly/3lXyFNt.

Remollino, A. (1905). *Documentos Interesantes de la Iglesia Filipina Independiente*. Manila: Imprenta Fajardo.

Remollino, A. (1926). *Réplica a la Obra del Fr. Cándido García Fernández Titulada "La Doctrina de la Iglesia Filipina Independiente: Exposición y Crítica"*. Manila: Imprenta Fajardo.

Retana y Gamboa, W.E. (1908). La Iglesia Filipina Independiente: Sin Nuevo Cisma Religioso. *Por Esos Mundos*. Madrid, 347-360.

Revollido, E.J. (2009). *The Interplay of Nationalism and Ecumenism in the Ministry of the Nine Supreme Bishops of the IFI: 1902-2002*. Ph.D. Dissertation. Manila: University of Santo Tomas.

Revollido, E.J. (2010). A Biographical Sketch of Supreme Bishop Gregorio Aglípay y Labayán. bit.ly/350dSlq.

Riggs, A.S. (1903, August). A Letter from the Philippines. *The Atlantic Monthly, 92*(550), 256-266.

Rivera, J. (1937, December). The Aglipayan Movement. *Philippine Social Science Review, 9*(4), 301-328.

Rivera, J. (1938, January). The Aglipayan Movement. *Philippine Social Science Review, 10*(1), 9-34).

Robertson, J.A. (1918, October). The Aglipayan Schism in the Philippine Islands. *The Catholic Historical Review*, 4(3), 315-344.

Rodell, P.A. (1988). The Founding of the Iglesia Filipina Independiente (the "Aglipayan" Church): An Historiographical Review. *Philippine Quarterly of Culture and Society*, 16(3-4), 210-234.

Rodríguez, I.R. (1960). *Gregorio Aglipay y los Orígenes de la Iglesia Filipina Independiente* (1898-1917). 2 vols. Madrid: Departamento de Misionología Espaniola, Consejo Superior de Investigaciones Cientificas.

Rosal, N.L.I. (1959). *Aglipayanism, Yesterday and Today*. Manila: University of St. Tomas Press.

Ruiz, J.M. (1950). *Three Pillars of the Philippine Independent Church*. Manila: Villamor.

Salamanca, B.S. (1968). *The Filipino Reaction to American Rule, 1901-1913*. Hamdon, CT: The Shoe String Press.

Salgado, G.G. (1978, March). *The Dynamics of Aglipayan-Catholic Confrontation in a Cebuano Community: Santa Fe, Cebu (1903-1953)*. M.A. thesis. Cebu City: University of San Carlos,

Schumacher, J.N. (1981). *Revolutionary Clergy: The Filipino Clergy and the Nationalist Movement, 1850-1903*. Quezon City: Ateneo de Manila University Press.

Scott, W.H. (1962, January). The Philippine Independent Church in History. *The East and West Review*, 28(1), 3-13.

Scott, W.H. (1963, July-September). The Philippine Independent Church in History. *Silliman Journal, 10*(3): 298-310. [A reprint of his 1962 article]

Scott, W.H. (1987). *Aglipay before Aglipayanism*. Quezon City: Aglipayan Resource Center.

Segbers, F., & Smit, P.B. (2011). Catholicity in times of globalization: Remembering Alberto Ramento, martyred bishop of workers and peasants. Luzern: Exodus.

Shirley, S. (2004). *Guided By God: The Legacy of the Catholic Church in Philippine Politics*. Singapore: Marshall Cavendish Academic.

Silva, S. (1903, April 23). Letter to Gregorio Aglipay. Quezon City: St. Andrew's Theological Seminary IFI Archive, OL 1462.

Silva, S. (1903, July 11). Letter to José Evangelista. Quezon City: St. Andrew's Theological Seminary IFI Archive, OL 1465.

Sison, J.C. (1941). *Crítica y Validez de los Sacramentos en la Iglesia Aglipayana*. Unpublished Doctoral Dissertation. Manila: Universidad de Santo Tomas.

Smit, P.B. (2011). *Old Catholic and Philippine Independent Ecclesiologies in History: The Catholic Church in Every Place (Brill's Series in Church History, 52)*. Leiden: Brill.

Smit, P.B. (2013). Von Kolonialkirche zur indigenen Theologie. Die Geschichte der Iglesia Filipina Independiente anhand ihrer Interpretation der Bibel [From colonial church to indigenous theology. The history of the Iglesia Filipina Independiente on the basis of its interpretation of the Bible]. *Jahrbuch fur europäische Überseegeschichte* [Yearbook of *European Overseas History*], 11,95-115.

Smit, P.B. (2014). The Philippine Independent Church. *World Book Encyclopedia*. www.worldbookonline.com.

Smit, P.B. (April 2015). From Antipodes to a Communion that Spans the Ends of the Earth. *The Christian Register: The Official Magazine of the Iglesia Filipina Independiente*, 10-11.

Smit, P.B. (2017). Contextualizing the Contextual: A Note on the Revolutionary Exegesis of Gregorio L. Aglipay. *Philippine Studies: Historical and Ethnographic Viewpoints, 65*, 71-83.

Ty, L.O. (1940, September 7). *Gregorio Aglípay: Priest, Soldier, Politician.* Philippine Free Press

Vacas, F. (1957, April-June). Exposición y Crítica del Bautismo Aglipayano. Unitas, 30(2), 227-301.

Vacas, F. (1958, January-March). Exposición y Crítica del Bautismo Aglipayano. *Unitas, 31*(1), 5-76. [A reprint of Vacas' 1957 article]

Vercammen, J. (2012). Commemoration of Bishop Alberto Ramento. *Internationale Kirchliche Zeitschrift* [*International Church Journal*], *102*(4), 300-304. bit.ly/319J6m9.

Victoriano, E.L. (1960, April). What Aglipayans Believe. *Philippine Studies, 8*(2), 292-299.

Whitney, J.R. (1971, April). Philippine National Religion and the Philippine National Church, *Anglican Theological Review, 53*(2), 85-103.

Whittemore, L.B. (1961). *Struggle for Freedom: History of the Philippine Independent Church*. Greenwich: Seabury Press.

Wise, F.H. (1965). *The History of the Philippine Independent Church*. Dumaguete City: College of Theology of Silliman University. [This is the author's 1955 master's thesis]

Endnotes

[1] Coleman, A. (1899). *The Friars in the Philippines*. Boston: Marlier, Callanan & Company, 13.

[2] *Ibid.*, 14.

[3] *Ibid.*

[4] *Ibid.*, 22.

[5] Piedad-Pugay, C. A. (2012, September 5). The Two Faces of the 1872 Cavite Mutiny. National Historic Commission of the Philippines. bit.ly/2T7xfDn.

[6] *Ibid.*

[7] Rizal, J. *El Filibusterismo* (The Reign of Greed). Cited in Beltrán, M. C. Virginia Moreno's *The Onyx Wolf* (*Itim Asu*): The Long Wail of History, 1719-1969. In Patajo-Legasto, P., Ed. *Philippine Studies: Have We Gone Beyond St. Louis?* Quezon City: The University of the Philippines Press, p. 202.

[8] Andrés, B. (1896, August 28). Mount of Liberty Proclamation. Translated from Salazar, Z. (1994). *Agosto 29-30, 1896: ang pagsalakay ni Bonifacio sa Maynila.* Quezon City: Miranda.

[9] Aguinaldo, E. (1964). *Mga gunita ng himagsikan, Manila.* Detroit: C. Aguinaldo Suntay.

[10] "President McKinley gives his reasons for the U.S. to keep the Philippines." bit.ly/2FB2JyT.

[11] Doeppers, D.F. (1976, April). The Philippine Revolution and the Geography of Schism. *Geographical Review, 66*(2), 159.

[12] *Ibid.*

[13] *Ibid.*, 161

[14] *Ibid.*, 163

[15] Coleman, A. (1899). *The Friars in the Philippines*. Boston: Marlier, Callanan & Company, 31.

[16] *Ibid.*, 37-38.

[17] *Ibid.*, 40-41.

[18] *Ibid.*, 43.

[19] *Ibid.*, 44.

[20] *Ibid.*, 56-57.

[21] *Ibid.*, 59.

[22] *Ibid.*

[23] *Ibid.*, 37-38.

[24] *Ibid.*, 62.

[25] *Ibid.*

[26] *Ibid.*, 63.

[27] *Ibid.*

[28] *Ibid.*, 64.

[29] *Ibid.*, 67.

[30] *Ibid.*, 69.

[31] *Ibid.*, 70.

[32] *Ibid.*, 69-70.

[33] *Ibid.*, 74-75.

[34] *Ibid.*, 75.

[35] *Ibid.*, 77-78.

[36] *Ibid.*, 80.

[37] *Ibid.*, 83.

[38] *Ibid.*, 87.

[39] *Ibid.*, 88.

[40] IFI History Committee (2011, June 8). Celebrating the Heritage for National Freedom, Independence and Abundant Life: A Historical Sketch. bit.ly/3lRu3Ip.

[41] Mojares, R. (2006). *Brains of the Nation: Pedro Paterno, T.H. Pardo de Tavera, Isabelo de los Reyes, and the Production of Modern Knowledge.* Quezon City: Ateneo de Manila University Press, 270.

[42] Agoncillo, T. (1990). *History of the Filipino people* (8th ed.). Quezon City: Garotech, 236-237.

[43] *Jamestown Weekly Alert.* (1901, February 28). Jamestown, North Dakota, 6.

[44] *The Leavenworth Times.* (1902, April 18). Leavenworth, Kansas, 5.

[45] *The Leaf-Chronicle.* (1902, May 29). Clarksville, Tennessee, 2

[46] *Santa Cruz Sentinel.* (1902, June 12). Santa Cruz, California, 1.

[47] *Ibid.*

[48] *The Los Angeles Times.* (1902, August 11). Los Angeles, California, 2.

[49] *Halstead Independent.* (1902, August 28). Halstead, Kansas, 2. Also in *The Dexter Advocate.* (1902, August 29). Dexter, Kansas, 6.

[50] Scott, W.H. (1962, January). The Philippine Independent Church in History. *East and West Review, 28*(1), 3-13.

[51] *The Buffalo Times.* (1902, August 11). Buffalo, New York, 8.

[52] Revollido, E.J. (2010). A Biographical Sketch of Supreme Bishop Gregorio Aglípay y Labayán. bit.ly/350dSlq.

[53] Scott, W.H. (1987). *Aglípay before Aglipayanism*. Quezon City: National Priests Organization.

[54] Revollido, E.J. (2010). A Biographical Sketch of Supreme Bishop Gregorio Aglípay y Labayán. bit.ly/350dSlq.

[55] Scott, W.H. (1987), 12.

[56] *Ibid.*, 18.

[57] Doeppers, D. F. (1976, April). The Philippine Revolution and the Geography of Schism. *Geographical Review, 66*(2), 162.

[58] de Achútegui, P.S. & Bernad, M.A. (1960). *Religious Revolution in the Philippines, Vol. III*. Manila: Ateneo de Manila, 92-3.

[59] Wenger, T. (2017). *Religious Freedom: The Contested History of an American Ideal*. Chapel Hill: University of North Carolina Press, 66.

[60] Doeppers, 164.

[61] Wenger, T. (2017). *Religious Freedom: The Contested History of an American Ideal*. Chapel Hill: University of North Carolina Press, 59.

[62] 1899 Constitution of the Republic of the Philippines (Malolos Convention). bit.ly/3k7m8WZ.

[63] Wenger, T. (2017). *Religious Freedom: The Contested History of an American Ideal*. Chapel Hill: University of North Carolina Press, 61-62.

[64] *Ibid.*, 65.

[65] Doeppers, 164.

[66] Revollido, E.J. (2010). A Biographical Sketch of Supreme Bishop Gregorio Aglípay y Labayán. bit.ly/350dSlq.

[67] Schumacher, J.N. (1992). *Revolutionary Clergy: The Filipino Clergy and the Nationalist Movement, 1850-1903*. Quezon City: New Day, 35.

[68] Reilly, H.J. (1900). *Annual Reports of the War Department for the Fiscal Year Ended June 30, 1900*, Vol. 3. Cited in W.H. Scott, 35.

[69] U.S. Military History Institute. (1900, April 1). *Spanish-American War Survey: Milton G. Nixon Family Correspondence*. Cited in W.H. Scott, 37.

[70] *The Evening Democrat*. (1900, July 4). Warren, Pennsylvania, 2.

[71] de Achútegui, P.S. & Bernad, M.A. (1960). *Religious Revolution in the Philippines, Vol. III*. Manila: Ateneo de Manila, 95.

[72] *Ibid.*, 98.

[73] Scott, 35.

[74] Wenger, T. (2017). *Religious Freedom: The Contested History of an American Ideal*. Chapel Hill: University of North Carolina Press, 68.

[75] Scott, 39.

[76] Stuntz, H.C. (1903, April 16). The Philippine Independent Church. *The Christian Advocate*, 623.

[77] Ranche, A.M. (n.d.). An Introduction to the Iglesia Filipina Independiente. bit.ly/3lXyFNt.

[78] *Ibid.*

[79] Balik Tanaw para sa Ika 113 Anibersaryo ng Iglesia Filipina Independiente. bit.ly/3j6jzmE.

[80] Cabillas, D.M. (2002, July). Iglesia Filipina Independiente (IFI): Comments from Churches Involved in Union Negotiations. *The Ecumenical Review*, 54(3).

[81] *Ibid.*

[82] Halili, M.C.N. (2010). *Philippine History*. Self-published.

[83] Cited in Wenger, T. (2017). *Religious Freedom: The Contested History of an American Ideal*. Chapel Hill: University of North Carolina Press, 72.

[84] Wenger, T. (2017). *Religious Freedom: The Contested History of an American Ideal*. Chapel Hill: University of North Carolina Press, 72.

[85] de los Reyes, I., Jr. (1948, June). The Iglesia Filipina Independiente (Philippine Independent Church): A Brief History. *Historical Magazine of the Protestant Episcopal Church, 17*, 133.

[86] Stuntz, H.C. (1903, April 16). The Philippine Independent Church. *The Christian Advocate*, 624.

[87] Stuntz, H.C. (1903, April 16). The Philippine Independent Church. *The Christian Advocate*, 623.

[88] Wenger, T. (2017). *Religious Freedom: The Contested History of an American Ideal*. Chapel Hill: University of North Carolina Press, 74.

[89] Aglípay, G. (1905). *Catecismo de la Iglesia Filipina Independiente*. Manila: Fajardo y Compañía, 46. bit.ly/3k96MkM.

[90] IFI History Committee (2011, June 8). Celebrating the Heritage for National Freedom, Independence and Abundant Life: A Historical Sketch. bit.ly/3lRu3Ip.

[91] *Ibid.*

[92] *Ibid.*

[93] Cited in Wenger, T. (2017). *Religious Freedom: The Contested History of an American Ideal*. Chapel Hill: University of North Carolina Press, 73.

[94] Stuntz, H.C. (1903, April 16). The Philippine Independent Church. *The Christian Advocate*, 623.

[95] Lynch, F. (1956). Aglipayanism. In Eggan, F., et al. (Eds.), *Area Handbook on the Philippines, 2*, Chicago, The University of Chicago Press. bit.ly/37dK2g4.

[96] *Ibid.*

[97] Stuntz, H.C. (1903, April 16). The Philippine Independent Church. *The Christian Advocate*, 624.

[98] de los Reyes, I., Sr. (1903, October 14). *La Iglesia Filipina Independiente Revista Católica, 1*(1), 1.

[99] El conflicto religioso. (1903, October 28). *La Patria, 2*(233).

[100] de los Reyes, I., Sr. (1903, November 1). Anemia de espíritu y de cabeza. *La Iglesia Filipina Independiente Revista Católica, 1*(4), 13.

[101] Notas…unidas. (1903, November 3). *Libertas, 5*(1267).

[102] de los Reyes. (1904, November 1). *La Iglesia Filipina Independiente Revista Católica, 2*(52), 205.

[103] Cited in Wenger, T. (2017). *Religious Freedom: The Contested History of an American Ideal*. Chapel Hill: University of North Carolina Press, 75.

[104] A Remarkable Religious Revival. (1903, March 19). *New Zealand Tablet, 31*(12), 17.

[105] That "Remarkable Religious Revival." (1903, March 26). *New Zealand Tablet, 31*(13), 17.

[106] That "Religious Revival." (1903, April 9). *New Zealand Tablet, 31*(15), 2.

[107] Cited in Wenger, T. (2017). *Religious Freedom: The Contested History of an American Ideal*. Chapel Hill: University of North Carolina Press, 75.

[108] *Ibid.*, 76.

[109] Wenger, T. (2017). *Religious Freedom: The Contested History of an American Ideal*. Chapel Hill: University of North Carolina Press, 77.

[110] de los Reyes, I., Sr. (1903, October 14). *La Iglesia Filipina Independiente Revista Católica, 1*(1), 3.

[111] Prautch, A.W. (1903, January 21). *La Verdad, 1*(1), 1.

[112] *Ibid.*, 16.

[113] Independent Catholics in Gao, India, and their Admirers, to Gregorio Aglipay. (1905, January 20). St. Andrew's Theological Seminary IFI Archive, OL 1491, O.M. 1.1, 1903-1905, Box 1, Aglipay-Herzog.

[114] Stuntz, H.C. (1903, April 16). The Philippine Independent Church. *The Christian Advocate*, 624.

[115] Lynch, F. (1956). Aglipayanism. In Eggan, F., et al. (Eds.), *Area Handbook on the Philippines, 2*, Chicago, The University of Chicago Press. bit.ly/37dK2g4.

[116] Wenger, T. (2017). *Religious Freedom: The Contested History of an American Ideal*. Chapel Hill: University of North Carolina Press, 73.

[117] Doeppers, D.F. (1976, April). The Philippine Revolution and the Geography of Schism. *Geographical Review, 66*(2), 164.

[118] Doeppers, D.F. (1976, April). The Philippine Revolution and the Geography of Schism. *Geographical Review, 66*(2), 164.

119 *Ibid.*, 167.

120 Stuntz, H.C. (1903, April 16). The Philippine Independent Church. *The Christian Advocate*, 623.

121 Kelly, P. (2016, May/August). Excavating a Hidden Bell Story from the Philippines: A Revised Narrative of Cultural-Linguistic Loss and Recuperation. *Journal of Folklore Research*, 53(2), 102-103.

122 *Ibid.*, 103-106.

123 *Ibid.*, 105.

124 de la Costa, H. (1967). Asia and the Philippines. Manila: Solidaridad Publishing, 144.

125 Wenger, T. (2017). *Religious Freedom: The Contested History of an American Ideal*. Chapel Hill: University of North Carolina Press, 68.

126 Doeppers, D.F. (1976, April). The Philippine Revolution and the Geography of Schism. *Geographical Review, 66*(2), 169.

127 Wenger, T. (2017). *Religious Freedom: The Contested History of an American Ideal*. Chapel Hill: University of North Carolina Press, 73.

128 *The Catholic Advance.* (1909 August 28), 5.

129 *Ibid.*

130 Stuntz, H.C. (1903, April 16). The Philippine Independent Church. *The Christian Advocate*, 624.

131 *Ibid.*

132 *Ibid.*

133 "Philippine Independent Church." bit.ly/2FyvUlY.

134 Aglípay, G. (1905). *Catecismo de la Iglesia Filipina Independiente*. Manila: Fajardo y Compañía, 37. bit.ly/3k96MkM.

135 Ranche, A.M. (n.d.). An Introduction to the Iglesia Filipina Independiente. bit.ly/3lXyFNt.

136 Cabillas, D.M. (2002, July). Iglesia Filipina Independiente (IFI): Comments from Churches Involved in Union Negotiations. *The Ecumenical Review, 54*(3).

137 Gealogo, F.A. (2010). Time, Identity, and Nation in the Aglipayan Novenario ng Balintawak and Calendariong Maanghang. *Philippine Studies 58*(1-2), 150-151.

138 Aglípay G. (1926). Novenary of the Motherland. Manila. bit.ly/3554RaL.

139 Ocampo, A.R. (2012, May 29). Virgin of Balintawak. bit.ly/34483nA.

140 *Iowa City Daily Press.* (1904, August 31). Iowa City, Iowa, 2.

141 Lynch, F. (1956). Aglipayanism. In Eggan, F., et al. (Eds.), *Area Handbook on the Philippines, 2*, Chicago, The University of Chicago Press. bit.ly/37dK2g4.

142 Stuntz, H.C. (1903, April 16). The Philippine Independent Church. *The Christian Advocate*, 624.

143 IFI History Committee (2011, June 8). Celebrating the Heritage for National Freedom, Independence and Abundant Life: A Historical Sketch. bit.ly/3lRu3Ip.

144 Aglípay, G. (1905). *Catecismo de la Iglesia Filipina Independiente*. Manila: Fajardo y Compañía, 46. bit.ly/3k96MkM.

145 de los Reyes. (1906). *Oficio Divino de la Iglesia Filipina Independiente*, Barcelona.

146 *Ibid.*, 3.

147 Lynch, F. (1956). Aglipayanism. In Eggan, F., et al. (Eds.), *Area Handbook on the Philippines, 2*, Chicago, The University of Chicago Press. bit.ly/37dK2g4.

148 Aglípay, G. (1905). *Catecismo de la Iglesia Filipina Independiente*. Manila: Fajardo y Compañía, 5. bit.ly/3k96MkM.

149 *Ibid.*, 8-10.

150 Lynch, F. (1956). Aglipayanism. In Eggan, F., et al. (Eds.), *Area Handbook on the Philippines, 2*, Chicago, The University of Chicago Press. bit.ly/37dK2g4.

151 Aglípay, G. (1905). *Catecismo de la Iglesia Filipina Independiente*. Manila: Fajardo y Compañía, 15. bit.ly/3k96MkM.

152 *Ibid.*, 19.

153 *Ibid.*, 21.

154 *Ibid.*, 24.

155 *Ibid.*, 28.

156 *Ibid.*, 30.

157 Wenger, T. (2017). *Religious Freedom: The Contested History of an American Ideal*. Chapel Hill: University of North Carolina Press, 80.

158 Project Canterbury. (1947). Correspondence and Other Papers Relating to the Petition of the Philippine Independent Church to the Protestant Episcopal Church in the U.S.A. for the Episcopal Consecration of Its Bishops. bit.ly/2Iw1L80.

159 Lynch, F. (1956). Aglipayanism. In Eggan, F., et al. (Eds.), *Area Handbook on the Philippines, 2*, Chicago, The University of Chicago Press. bit.ly/37dK2g4.

160 Lim, D. (1989). Church and State in the Philippines, 1900-1988. *Transformation*, 6(3), 27.

161 Doeppers, D.F. (1976, April). The Philippine Revolution and the Geography of Schism. *Geographical Review*, 66(2), 166.

162 de Archutegui, P.S. & Bernad, M.A. (1964, July). The Aglipayan Churches and the Census of 1960. Philippine Studies, 12(3), 446.

163 Doeppers, D.F. (1976, April). The Philippine Revolution and the Geography of Schism. *Geographical Review, 66*(2), 167.

164 de Archutegui, P.S. & Bernad, M.A. (1964, July). The Aglipayan Churches and the Census of 1960. Philippine Studies, 12(3), 446.

165 *Hammond Times.* (1935, September 3). Hammond, Indiana, 14.

166 *Ibid.*

167 *Ibid.*

168 *San Antonio Express.* (1935, September 17). San Antonio, Texas, 2.

169 *San Antonio Express.* (1935, June 7). San Antonio, Texas, 8.

170 *San Antonio Express.* (1935, July 13). San Antonio, Texas, 6.

171 *Oakland Tribune.* (1935, August 9). Oakland, California, B12.

172 *Hammond Times.* (1935, September 3). Hammond, Indiana, 14.

173 *Boyden Reporter.* (1935, September 26). Boyden, Iowa, 1. Also in *Fredericksburg News.* (1935, October 3). Fredericksburg, Iowa, 3.

174 *El Paso Herald-Post.* (1935, September 18). El Paso, Texas, 1.

175 *Fitchburg Sentinel.* (1935, November 19). Fitchburg, Massachusetts, 6.

176 *Hamilton Daily News Journal.* (1935, September 21). Hamilton, Ohio, 6.

177 *San Antonio Express.* (1935, September 19). San Antonio, Texas, 8.

178 *San Antonio Express.* (1935, July 3). San Antonio, Texas, 8.

179 *San Antonio Express.* (1936, June 3). San Antonio, Texas, 2.

180 *Ibid.*

181 *Ogden Standard Examiner.* (1938, January 27). Ogden, Utah, 10.

182 IFI Facebook page. (2014, March 30). bit.ly/34YzfmY.

183 de Achútegui, P.S. & Bernad, M.A. (1960). *Religious Revolution in the Philippines, Vol. I.* Manila: Ateneo de Manila, 500.

184 Ty, L.O. (1940, September 7). *Gregorio Aglípay: Priest, Soldier, Politician.* Philippine Free Press, 36-37.

185 *Oakland Tribune.* (1941, November 7). Oakland, California, 31.

186 Quezón, M. (1940, September). Address at Bayan, Manila.

187 Ablan, R.B. (1940, September 15). Quoted by W.H. Scott in his message delivered for the commemoration of the 30th death anniversary of Bishop Aglípay, St. Andrew's Theological Seminary, Quezon City in September 1970.

188 *Fitchburg Sentinel.* (1942, January 3). Fitchburg, Massachusetts, 10.

[189] Yabes, L.Y. (1936). *A Brief Survey of Iloko Literature: From the Beginning to Its Present Development.* Manila: Self-published. bit.ly/2T0vvfd.

[190] Smit, P.B. (2011). *Old Catholic and Philippine Independent Ecclesiologies in History: The Catholic Church in Every Place (Brill's Series in Church History, 52).* Leiden: Brill, 335.

[191] *The Daily Courier.* (1940, November 19). Connellsville, Pennsylvania, 5. Also in *Dunkirk Evening Observer.* (1940, November 27). Dunkirk, New York, 3 and in *Mansfield News Journal.* (1940, November 21). Mansfield, Ohio, 18.

[192] Parpan, A.G. (1989). The Japanese and the Philippine Church, 1942-1945. *Philippine Studies, 37*(4), 460.

[193] IFI History Committee (2011, June 8). Celebrating the Heritage for National Freedom, Independence and Abundant Life: A Historical Sketch. bit.ly/3lRu3Ip.

[194] Cabillas, D.M. (2019, September 12). Is Reconciliation after "Separation" 54 Years Ago Still Possible? bit.ly/3nZMah9.

[195] *The Concord Times.* (1916, January 27). Concord, North Carolina, 2.

[196] *The Monclair Times.* (1931, May 30). Montclair, New Jersey, 19.

[197] IFI History Committee (2011, June 8). Celebrating the Heritage for National Freedom, Independence and Abundant Life: A Historical Sketch. bit.ly/3lRu3Ip.

[198] Ranche, A.M. (n.d.). An Introduction to the Iglesia Filipina Independiente. bit.ly/3lXyFNt.

[199] Smit, P.B. (2011). *Old Catholic and Philippine Independent Ecclesiologies in History: The Catholic Church in Every Place* (Brill's Series in Church History, 52). Leiden: Brill, 162.

[200] IFI website. bit.ly/3j71Ds8.

[201] Bureau of Census and Statistics. (1960). *Census of the Philippines, 1960: Population and Housing, 2,* 17.

[202] Bureau of Census and Statistics. (1970). *Census of the Philippines, 1970, 2,* Table III-18.

[203] de Archutegui, P.S. & Bernad, M.A. (1964, July). The Aglipayan Churches and the Census of 1960. *Philippine Studies, 12*(3), 446-459.

[204] de los Reyes, I., Jr. (1948, June). The Iglesia Filipina Independiente (Philippine Independent Church): A Brief History. *Historical Magazine of the Protestant Episcopal Church, 17,* 135.

[205] IFI website. bit.ly/3j71Ds8.

[206] IFI History Committee (2011, June 8). Celebrating the Heritage for National Freedom, Independence and Abundant Life: A Historical Sketch. bit.ly/3lRu3Ip.

[207] *Public Opinion* (1948, July 31). Chambersburg, Pennsylvania, 3.

[208] *Ibid.*

[209] O'Connor, P. (1947, November 29). *The Tablet*, 11.

[210] Project Canterbury. (1947). Correspondence and Other Papers Relating to the Petition of the Philippine Independent Church to the Protestant Episcopal Church in the U.S.A. for the Episcopal Consecration of Its Bishops. bit.ly/2Iw1L80.

[211] *Ibid.*

[212] *Ibid.*

[213] *Ibid.*

[214] *Ibid.*

[215] *Ibid.*

[216] *Ibid.*

[217] *Ibid.*

[218] *Ibid.*

[219] *Ibid.*

[220] *Ibid.*

[221] *Ibid.*

[222] *Paducah Sun-Democrat.* (1948, June 11). Paducah, Kentucky, 8.

[223] *Honolulu Star-Bulletin.* (1948, May 3). Honolulu, Hawaii, 10.

[224] *Shamokin News-Dispatch.* (1948, June 19). Shamokin, Pennsylvania, 5.

[225] IFI History Committee (2011, June 8). Celebrating the Heritage for National Freedom, Independence and Abundant Life: A Historical Sketch. bit.ly/3lRu3Ip.

[226] *The Honolulu Advertiser.* (1961, September 9). Honolulu, Hawaii, 7.

[227] *The Call-Leader.* (1961, October 27). Elwood, Indiana, 1.

[228] *Tampa Bay Time.* (1964, November 14). St. Petersburg, Florida, 46.

[229] *Eureka Humboldt Standard.* (1966, April 22). Eureka, California, 1.

[230] Padagas, E.J. (2017, December 8). Learning About the Aglipayan Church. bit.ly/3k4wln6.

[231] *Ibid.*

[232] *Ibid.*

[233] IFI History Committee (2011, June 8). Celebrating the Heritage for National Freedom, Independence and Abundant Life: A Historical Sketch. bit.ly/3lRu3Ip.

[234] Dayagbil, V.O. (n.d.). The Philippine Independent Catholic Church: A Brief History. bit.ly/353C1Yl.

235 IFI History Committee (2011, June 8). Celebrating the Heritage for National Freedom, Independence and Abundant Life: A Historical Sketch. bit.ly/3lRu3Ip.

236 *Ibid.*

237 *Ibid.*

238 *The Honolulu Advertiser.* (1976, July 17). Honolulu, Hawaii, 17.

239 IFI History Committee (2011, June 8). Celebrating the Heritage for National Freedom, Independence and Abundant Life: A Historical Sketch. bit.ly/3lRu3Ip.

240 *Ibid.*

241 *Edmonton Journal.* (1964, May 23). Edmondton, Alberta.

242 *Pacific Daily News.* (1989, August 7). Agana Heights, Guam, 4.

243 Vianzon, F.G. (1989, August 16). *Pacific Daily News.* Agana Heights, Guam, 35.

244 *Pacific Daily News.* (2006, October 5). Agana Heights, Guam, 14.

245 *Pacific Daily News.* (2006, October 14). Agana Heights, Guam, 43.

246 Araneta, S. & Bagares, R. (2000, April 7). Baba Case: Mistaken Identity. *PhilStar Global.* bit.ly/3dFcf0n.

247 Philippine Statistical Authority. (2015). *Philippines in Figures, 2015.* bit.ly/2T0GfKH.

248 Ellao, J.A.J. (2014, June 13). Tomas Millamena: Bishop of the people, staunch defender of justice and peace. *Bulatlat.* bit.ly/2HbkjtA.

249 *Ibid.*

250 *Ibid.*

251 *Ibid.*

252 *Ibid.*

253 *Ibid.*

254 *Iglesia Filipina Independiente* website. bit.ly/2GXhyfT.

255 Philippine Statistical Authority. (2015). *Philippine Statistical Yearbook, 2015.* bit.ly/ 37c4Rbw.

256 Taguba, C.T. (2011, August 18). Filipino Parish Netherlands Launched on the Occasion of Philippine Historical Events. *Munting Nayon: News & Views of the Filipino Community Worldwide.* bit.ly/342Xr8A.

257 Torres, J. & Tupas, J. (2016, January 7). Philippine Independent Church Denies Backing Late Dictator's Son. *Union of Catholic Asian News.* bit.ly/3dA7HZc.

258 Iglesia Filipina Independiente Asks Forgiveness from LGBT community, Extends Hand with Pro-equality Statement. (2017, August 31). *Outrage.* bit.ly/2FzhFgL.

259 *Ibid.*

260 Vergara, W. (2019, April 29). Philippine Independent Church Prepares to Consecrate First Woman Bishop. *Episcopal News Service.* bit.ly/3lULVSM.

261 *Ibid.*

262 Vergara, W. (2019, May 29). First Woman Bishop Makes History in Philippine Independent Church. *Episcopal News Service.* bit.ly/345nr37.

263 *Ibid.*

264 *Ibid.*

265 Nicastro, R. (1990, August 7). Philippine Independent Church Creates North American Diocese: New Questions Raised on Relationship with Anglican Communion. *Episcopal News Service.* bit.ly/3dyirai.

266 Philippine Statistical Authority. (2015). *Philippine Statistical Yearbook, 2015.* bit.ly/ 37c4Rbw.

267 World Council of Churches. bit.ly/3lZV8JP.

Index